I0485135

Inspired By Her

Celebrating Femininity through Art Quilts

Aisha Lumumba

Cover designed by Jamal Pope
from www.GreenlightDesignStudios.com

Cover quilt: Only Women Have Wings

Copyright © 2016 Aisha Lumumba

All rights reserved.

ISBN-13:978-0-9911305-3-5

I dedicate this book to all the Mothers that realized that I needed a mother and shared their love with me.

Mattie Pittman, Marion Daniel, Ann McMullen, Marion Cleveland, Dorothy Brown, Rosetta Hinton and Nellie Ruth McKibben

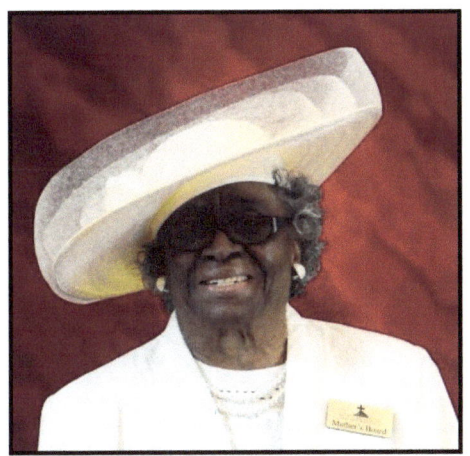

Mattie Pittman

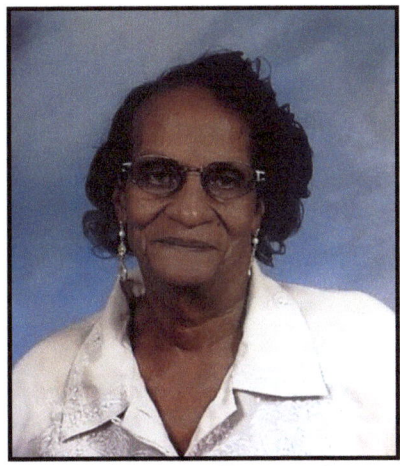

Marion Daniel

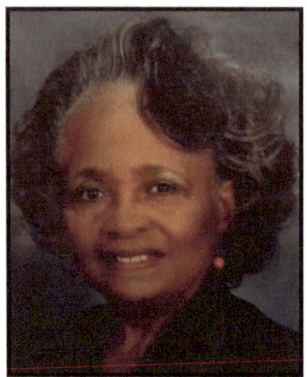

Ann McMullen

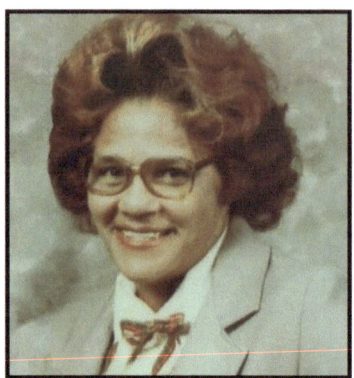

Marion Cleveland

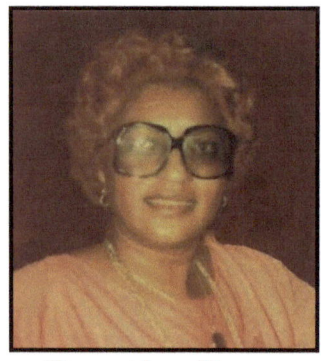

Dorothy Brown

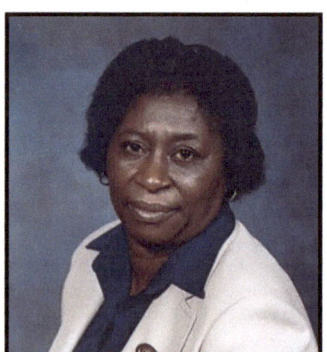

Rosetta Hinton

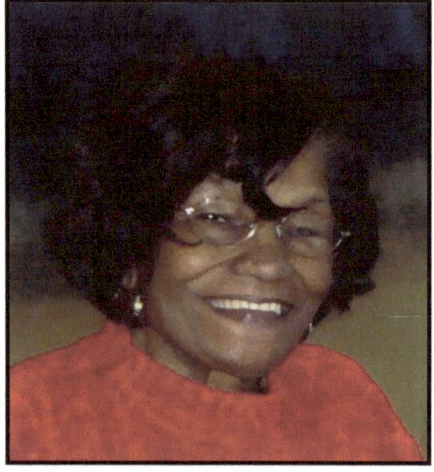

Nellie Ruth McKibben

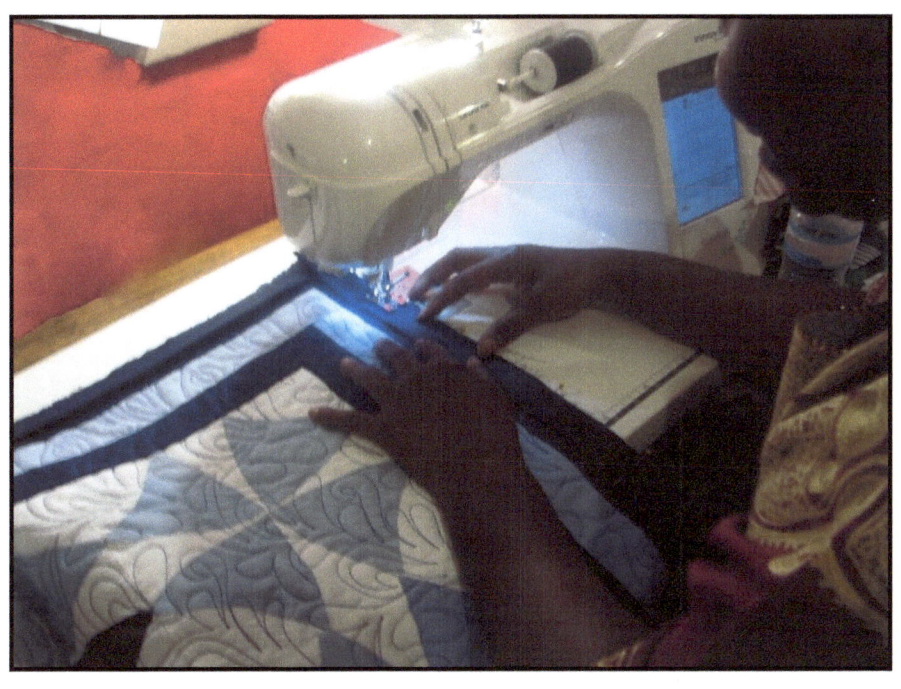

CONTENTS

Acknowledgments   i

1   She Loves Gumbo   5

2   She Is Steppin' Out   10

3   She Wears A Glorious Crown   17

4   She Is The Hair Revolution   28

5   She Is Legendary   33

6   She Is Dance   43

7   She Is Growing   50

8   She Has Wings   53

9   She Is A Musician   59

10   She Is Loved   63

11   She Is   67

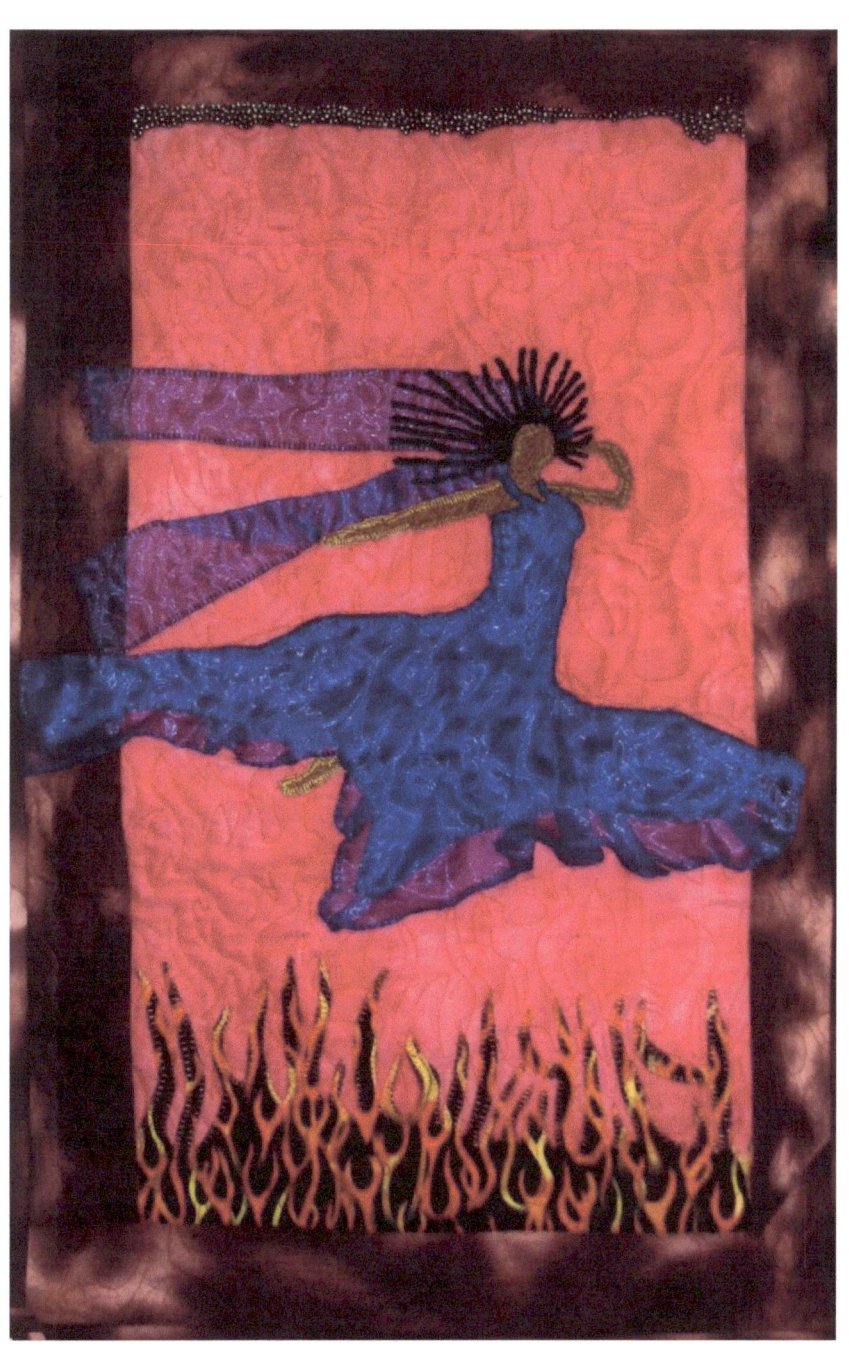

ACKNOWLEDGMENTS

I'd like to acknowledge all the people who have encouraged me to go on: my husband, my children and my very large family plus all my friends.

First and foremost I'd like to acknowledge Faith Ringgold for her bravery and foresight in bringing quilting to a high standard in the art community. I also want to thank the many portrait quilt artist who have inspired and influenced my work, namely Bisa Butler, Dawn Boyd-Williams, Janice Hollis-Sullivan, April Anue, Lola Jenkins, Phyllis Stephens, Nancy Cash, Alice Beasley and Ramsess.

Cookie Torreah Washington and Marla A. Jackson have been wonderful mentors. I want to say thanks to all the African American quilt artists from coast to coast who believe in this art form.

Special thanks to Greenlight Design Studios for the outstanding cover and design guidance. Undying thanks to Jabari Lumumba for being my number one photographer.

Loving thanks to Marquetta Johnson for creating lovely hand dyed fabrics that enhance so many of my quilts.

INTRODUCTION

Yes, I was inspired by Her. Men and women alike have played important roles in my life but the women have been the most powerful inspiration. The inspiration may be directly related to my being female and looking up to them in patterning my own life. Whatever the reason I was so inspired to be the best woman I could be.

Early in life my older sisters were central to my growth. I looked up to them and wanted to do everything they did, exactly like they did it. I learned to love, to dress myself, to hate getting my hair straightened and a host of other things from them. And my older cousins were there as well, and they had no idea that they too were setting an example for me. I was drinking in their actions with large gulps.

My aunts came next, each with their own beauty and talents. They never hesitated to express their ideas about beauty when I saw them and they clearly displayed their talents. Aunt Callie would enter the room and say, "The beautiful one has arrived. Everything can start now." Aunt Esther would say that she was fine as frog's hair, while Aunt Annie confessed that she couldn't help looking good because it ran in the family.

I learned to sew from a couple of them and learned to cook from others. I also learned a lot about disciplining children by being disciplined by them- some good and some not so good.

I had some really wonderful women teachers and counselors in my early school years. Plenty of book learning took place with them and a lot of self-esteem building as well. One of them even taught me the best way to care for my hair. My hair was soft and fine and very different from other people's hair. She told me that my hair could not take the amount of heat I was putting on it. She said as a matter of fact, you can do without the straightening comb. She was speaking my kind of language.

And least I forget- my best friends' mothers who took me in and treated me like their own when I visited with their daughters. They saw a need in me and fulfilled it. I am forever grateful to them and love them much.

By the time I reached adulthood, I still had all of those wonderful ladies to lean on. I called them often to get advice and visited when I could. Some gave advice when I didn't ask for it.

Good friends abound. I have a large number of really good sister friends who are now helping to set a fantastic example for my daughters. I feel blessed to have so many really good friends.

Now I want to make sure that other growing girls have the benefit of great feminine examples. Whereas my examples were in the flesh. I could have used more encouragement in the form of art and images. My struggle to find an abundance of art that reflected my life did not exist and that is why I set out to add to the body of African American art work.

So I present to you the culmination of women in art quilts doing some of the important things that have shaped my life. These quilts are ever evolving and so am I.

1

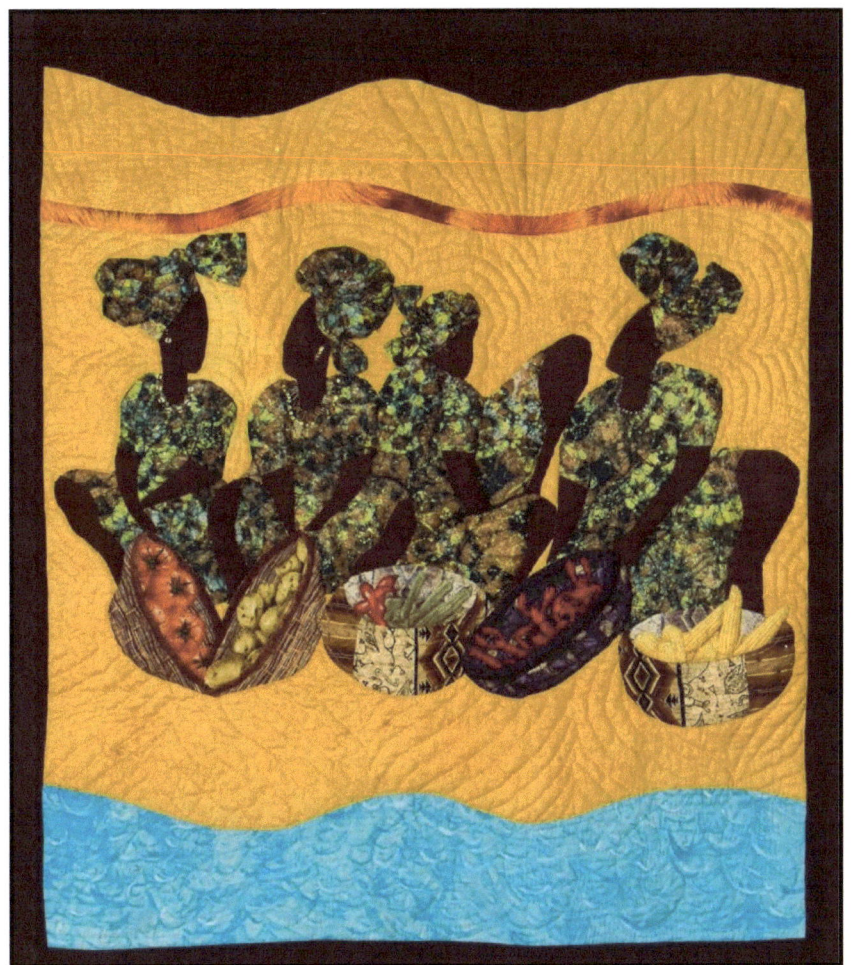

SHE LOVES GUMBO

These quilts were inspired by the idea of women making gumbo with a little bit of this and that. The style of this quilt was created at the beginning of my art quilt adventures.

Gumbo is a traditional dish originating in Africa and surviving the trip across the ocean through the Caribbean to Louisiana where it is a popular dish.

Gumbo became known as the delicious dish of the Louisiana Cajun and Creole people during the 18th century. It is usually made of a stock, okra, meat, chicken or shellfish, and seasoned vegetables, which could possibly include garlic, celery, bell peppers and onions. Gumbo most often uses the African vegetable okra, the Choctaw spice file' powder (dried and ground sassafras leaves), and roux (a thickener)- the French base made of flour and fat.

The dish was possibly named from the Bantu word for okra (ki ngombo) or the Choctaw word for file' (kombo) or maybe they understood each other.

I was so influenced by a story I heard that in certain African societies the women move through life stages together as an age group/generation; meaning that the people you go to school with, go through puberty with, get married around the same time, have children together and all other life celebrations together. It seemed to me like grouping people in generations. Each grouping has its own dress/outfit that identifies them. That is why I dressed all the women alike. The distinguishing difference is the way each one wrapped their head and distinct jewelry.

I love the art of basket weaving although I do not know how to do it. So the idea of sewing baskets and filling them with food fabric excited me. Gumbo came to mind because it is a traditional dish that brings together lots of vegetables and sometimes seafood. I envisioned that the ladies were gathering baskets of food for making gumbo.

The ribbon across the top was a gentle curve technique that I was taught by Marquetta Johnson. I continued the same technique with the water at the bottom of the quilt.

This quilt features many creative techniques such as appliqué, fabric painting, and beaded embellishments. Many variations of this quilt exist from students who have taken my workshop. I am so pleased to see their innovative results.

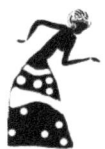

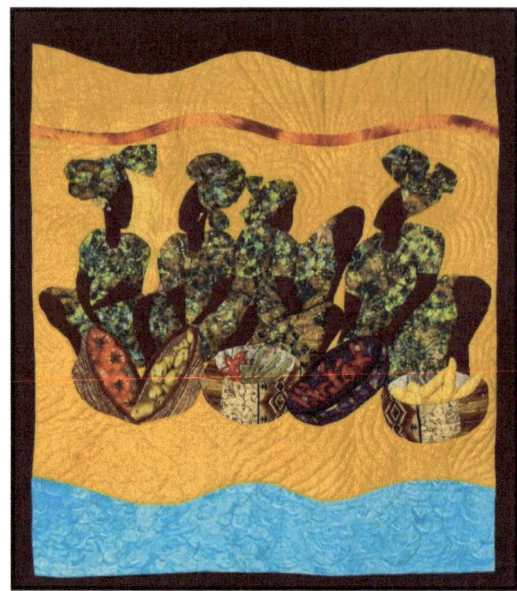

"Gumbo Ladies 1: A Bit Of This And That"
65" x 70"

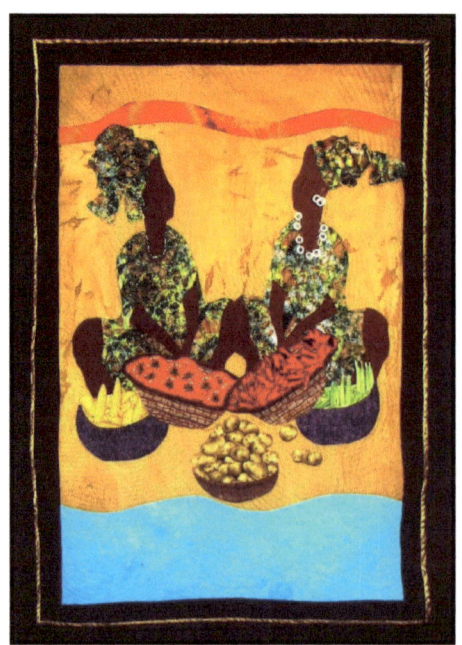

"Gumbo Ladies 2: Lagniappe Sill Vous Plait"
45" x 65"

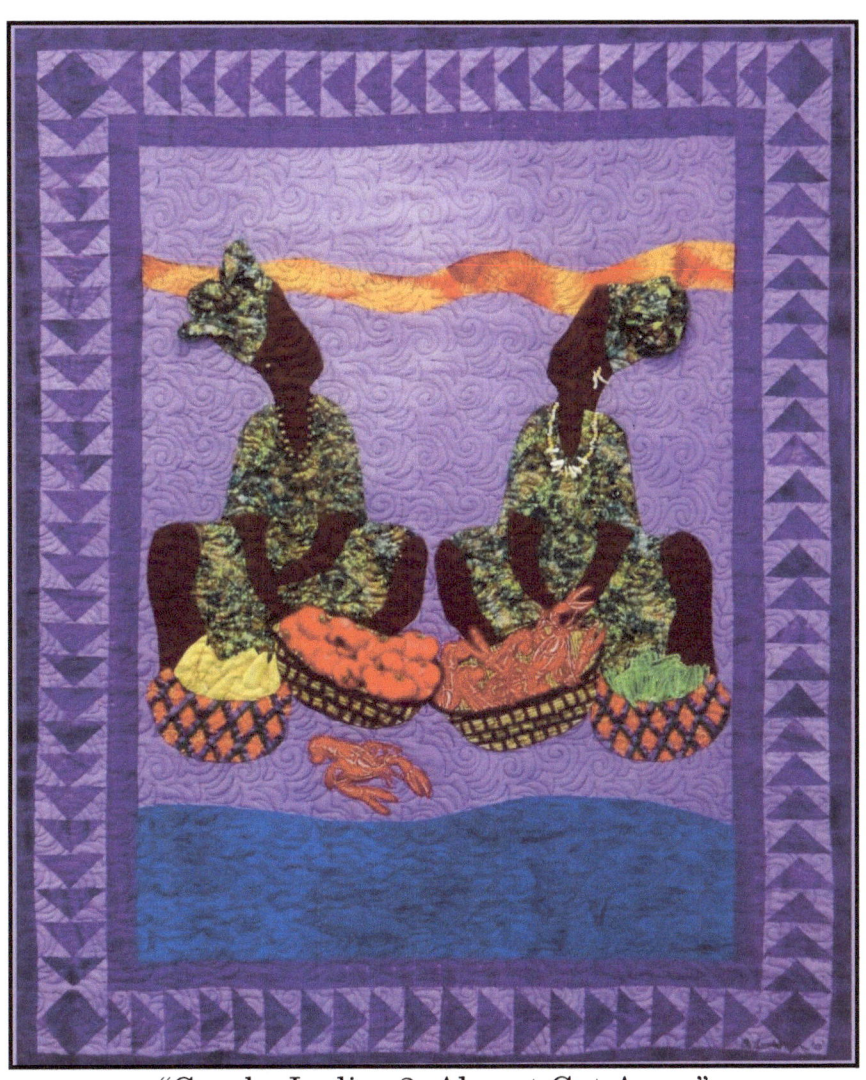

"Gumbo Ladies 3: Almost Got Away"
51" x 66"

2

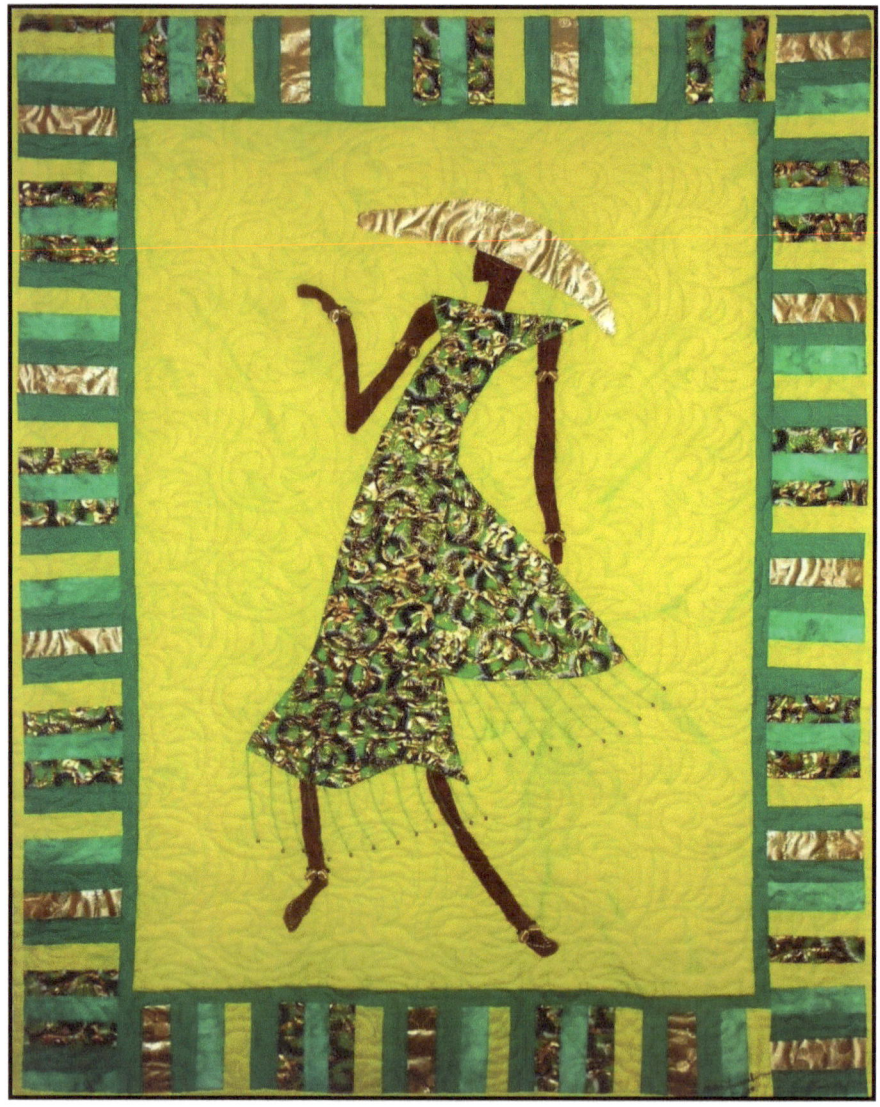

SHE IS STEPPIN' OUT

These quilts were created as a tribute to the lady that loves to dress up in a beautiful dress and "step out." She wears an oversized hat, extremely expressive jewelry with the daintiest earrings.

This quilt pattern was my first use of raw edge applique. I thought I didn't like it because I didn't like the idea of a "raggedy edge". When I started doing it, I fell in love. I didn't leave the edge ragged, I finished it off with either a satin stitch or a blanket stitch.

The first lady I made had on an orange dress because orange is my favorite color. I have found that I am among the few people that absolutely love orange.

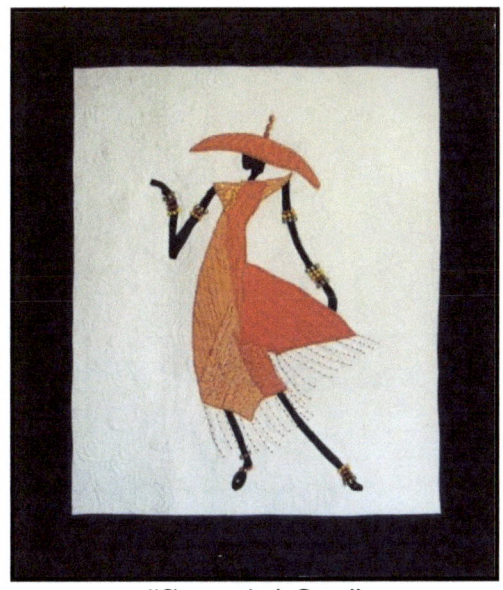

"Steppin' Out"
29" x 40"

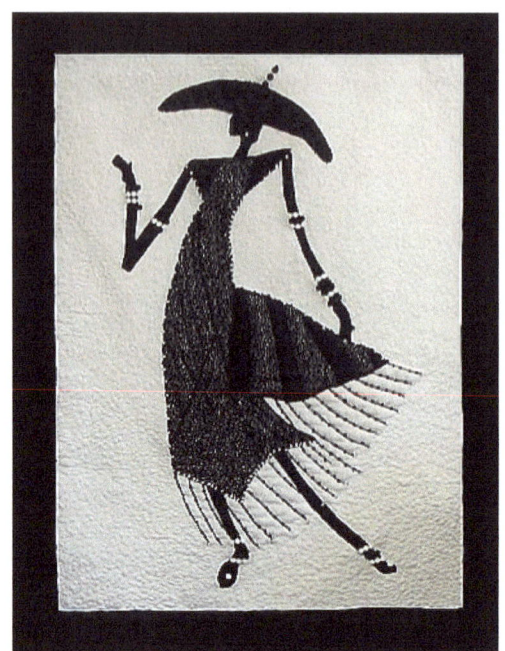

"Steppin' Out 2"
28" x 40"

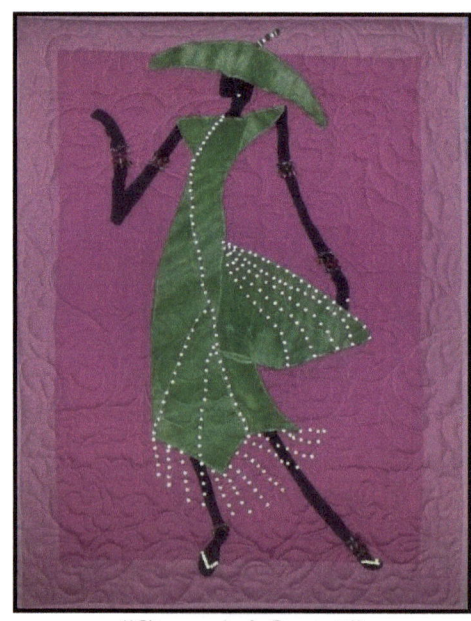

"Steppin' Out 3"
28" x 36"

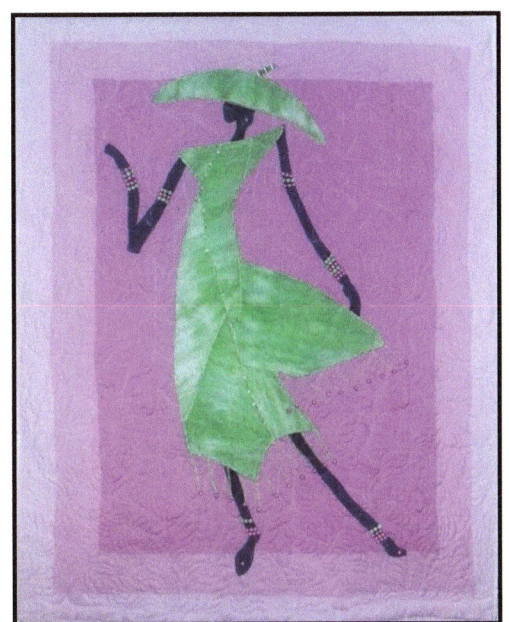

"Steppin' Out 4"
28" x 36"

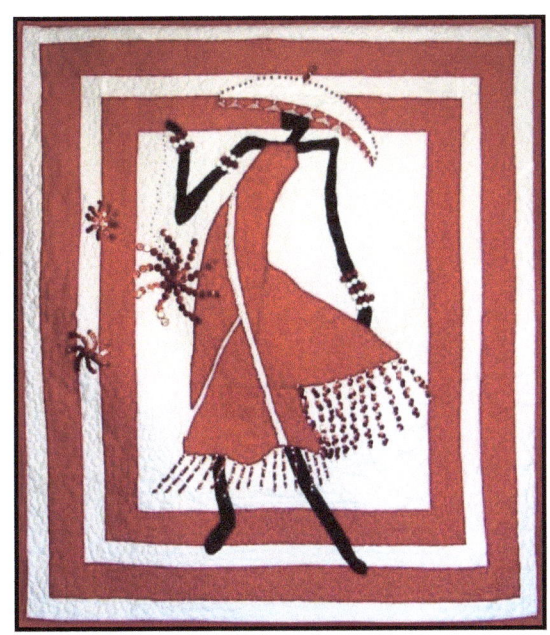

"Steppin' Out 6"
33" x 39"

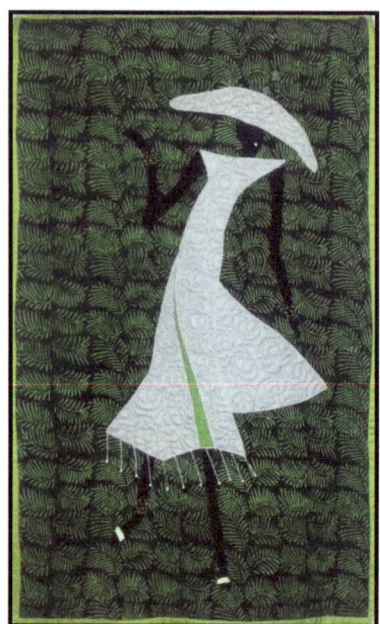

"Steppin' Out 7"
26" x 41"

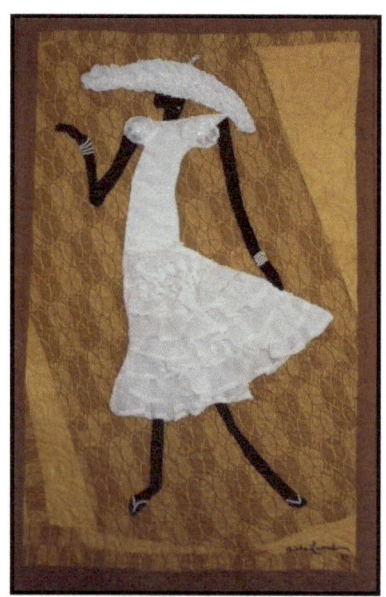

"Steppin' Out 8"
25" x 40"

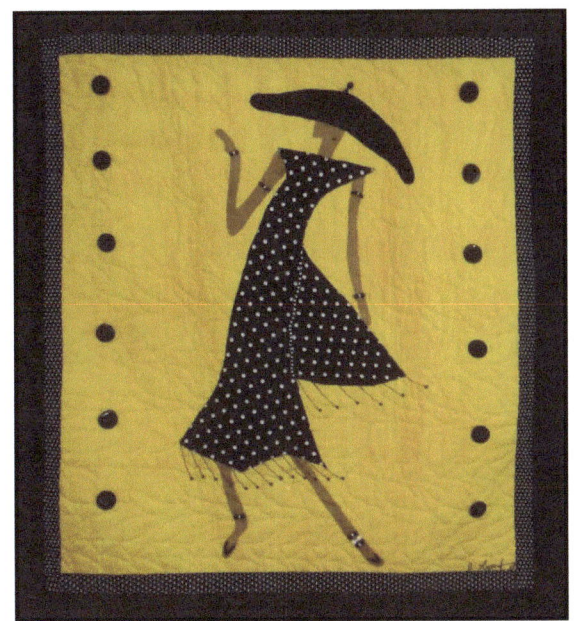

"Steppin' Out 9"
35" x 39"

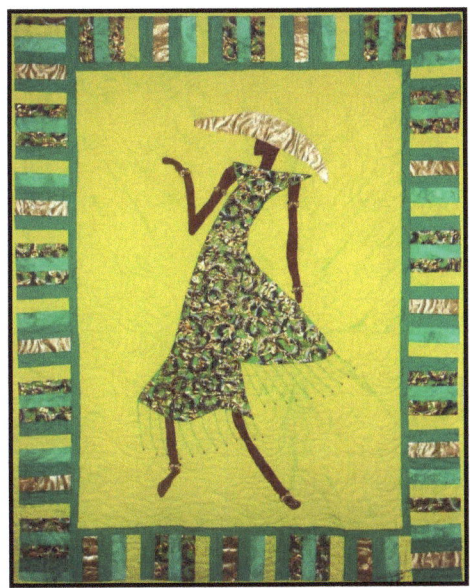

"Steppin' Out 10"
29" x 40"

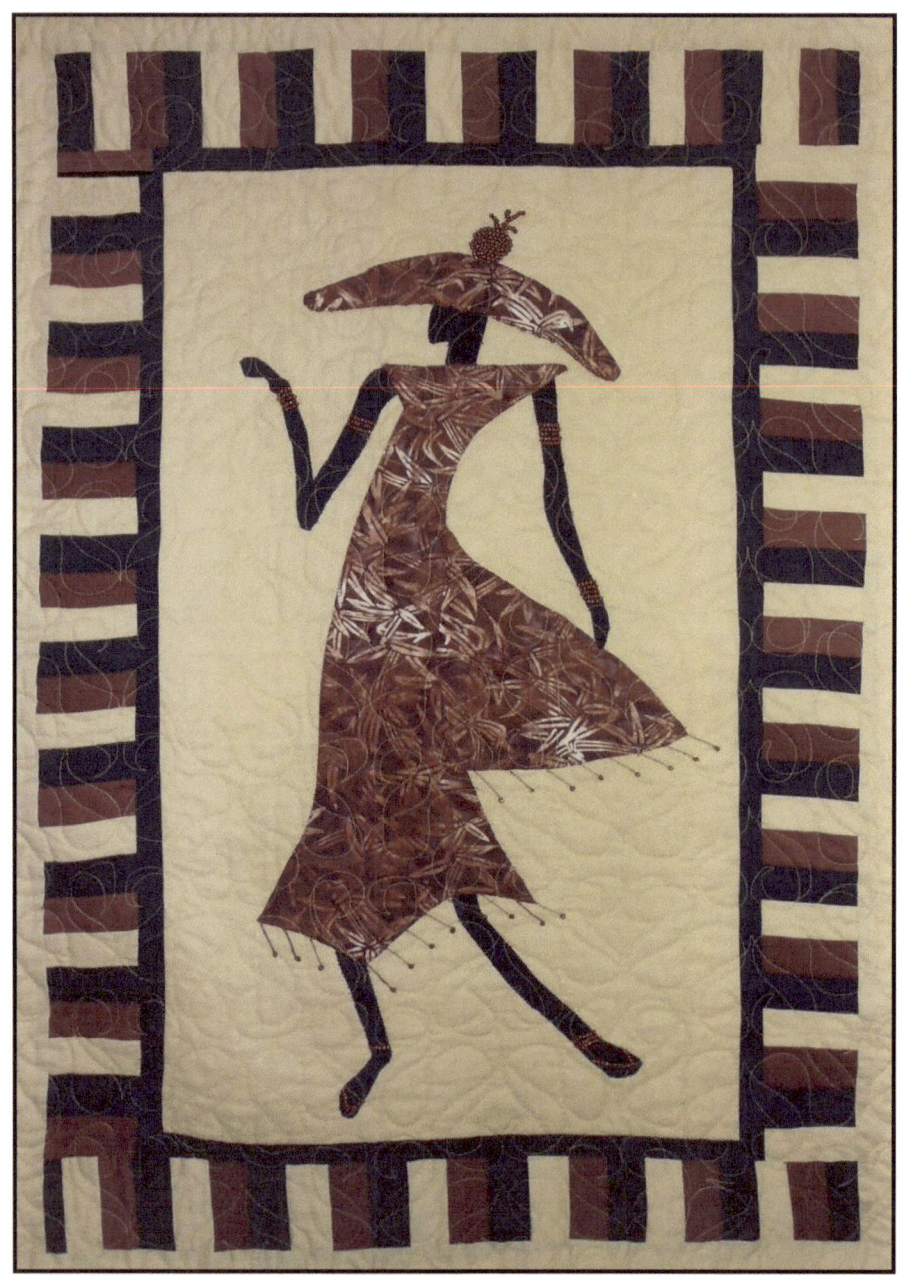

"Steppin' Out 11"
33" x 50"

3

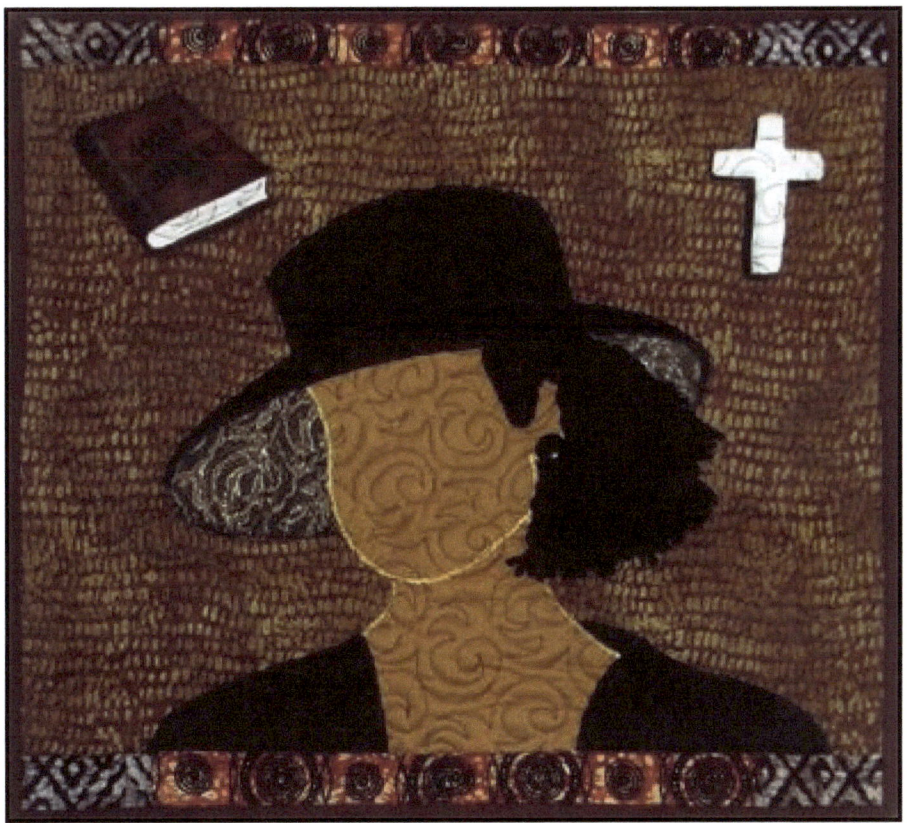

SHE WEARS A GLORIOUS CROWN

These quilts celebrate the tradition of African Americans wearing hats to church. Many women worked domestic jobs that required uniforms. Sunday was the day to express their beauty and hat flair. They wore elaborate hats and dressed beautifully on Sunday.

I offer that the tradition of wearing hats also stemmed from the African tradition of wrapping ones head with a beautiful head dress which often denoted social status. Church hats were also used as a symbol of status.

As the 1960's brought pride for natural hair styles which did not fit well under the hat, the hat tradition was continued mostly by older women.

Hair styles no longer prohibit the wearing of a hat. Now women of all ages wear hats on and over all hair styles.

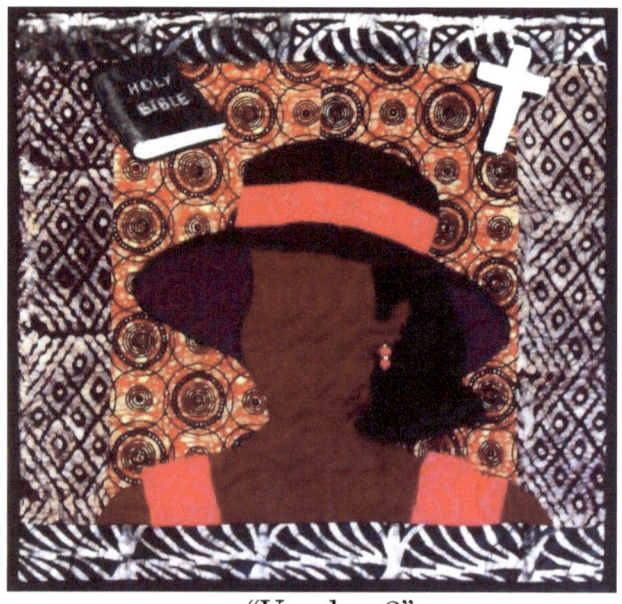

"Vendya 2"
22" x 28"

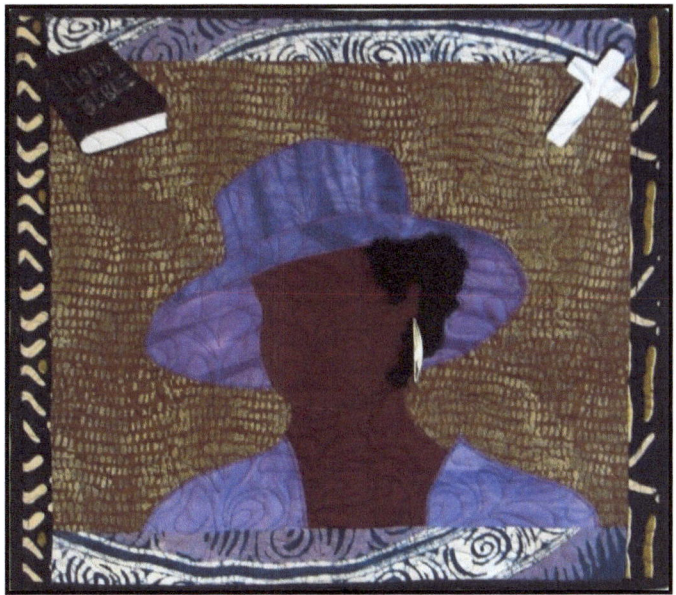

"Vendya 3"
21" x 28"

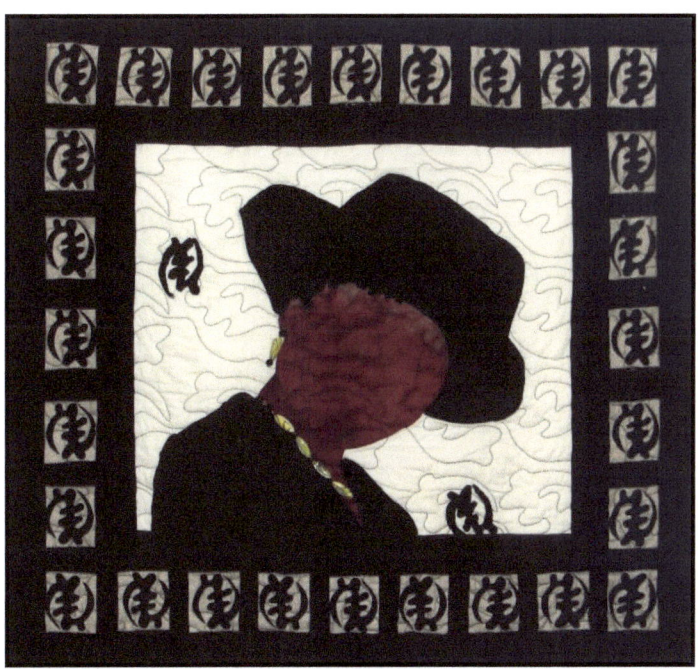

"Willow"
31" x 31"

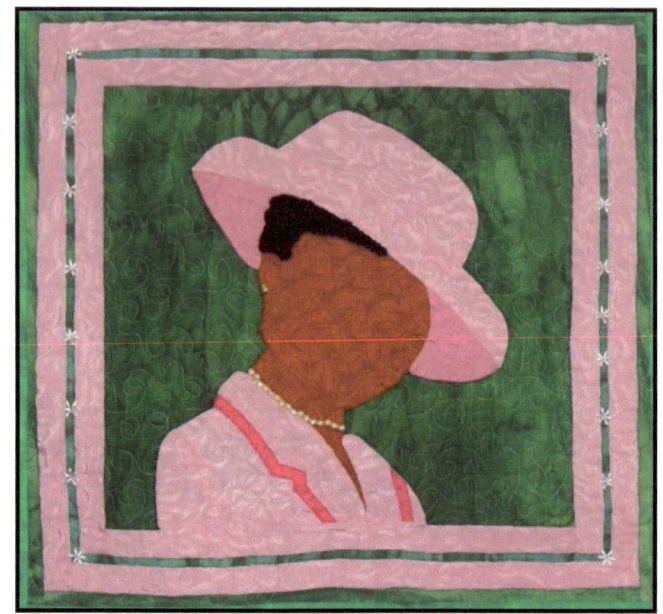

"Willow 2
31" x 31"

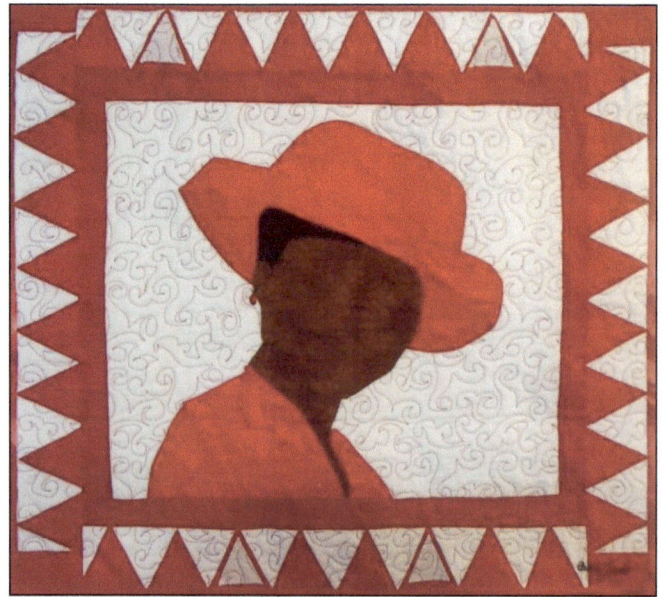

"Willow 3"
30" x 29"

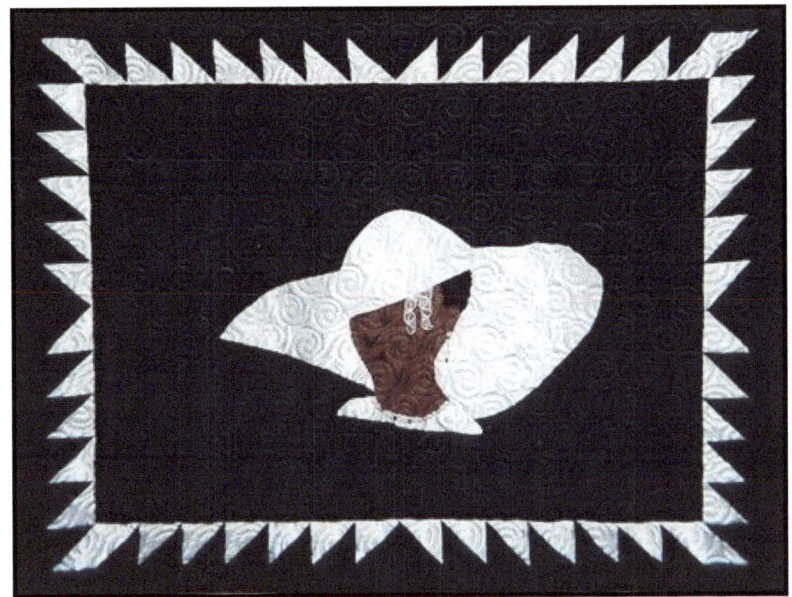

"Mrs. Big"
48" x 36"

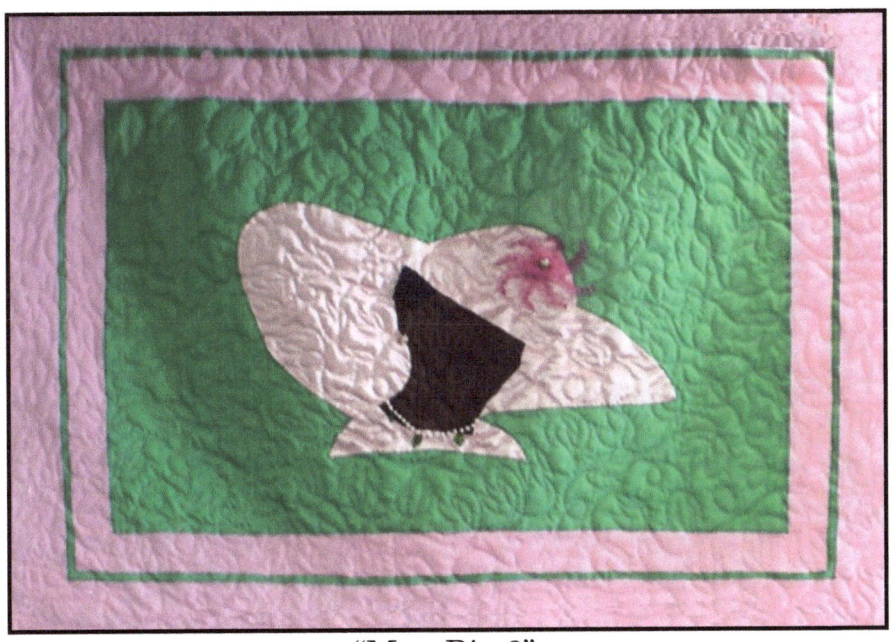

"Mrs. Big 3"
46" x 36"

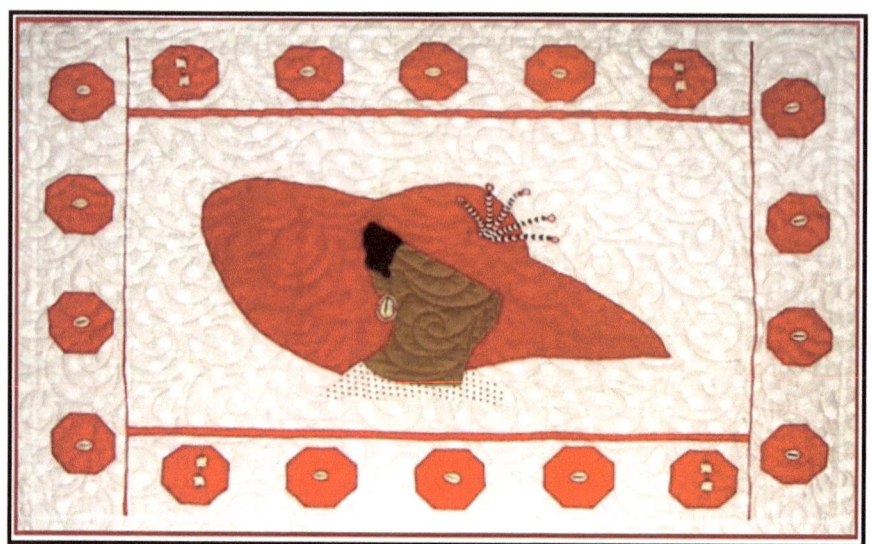

"Mrs. Big 5"
47" x 34"

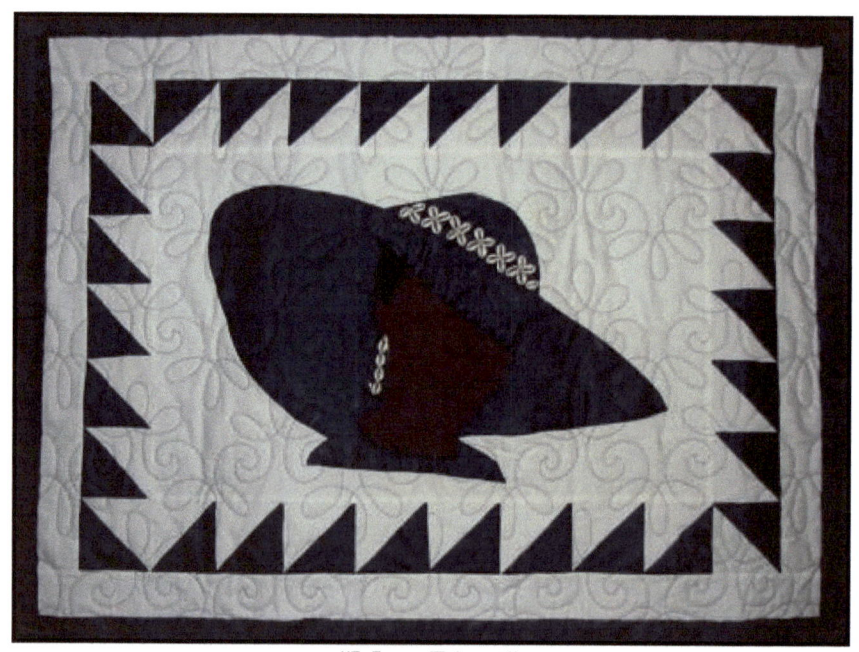

"Mrs. Big 6"
46" x 35"

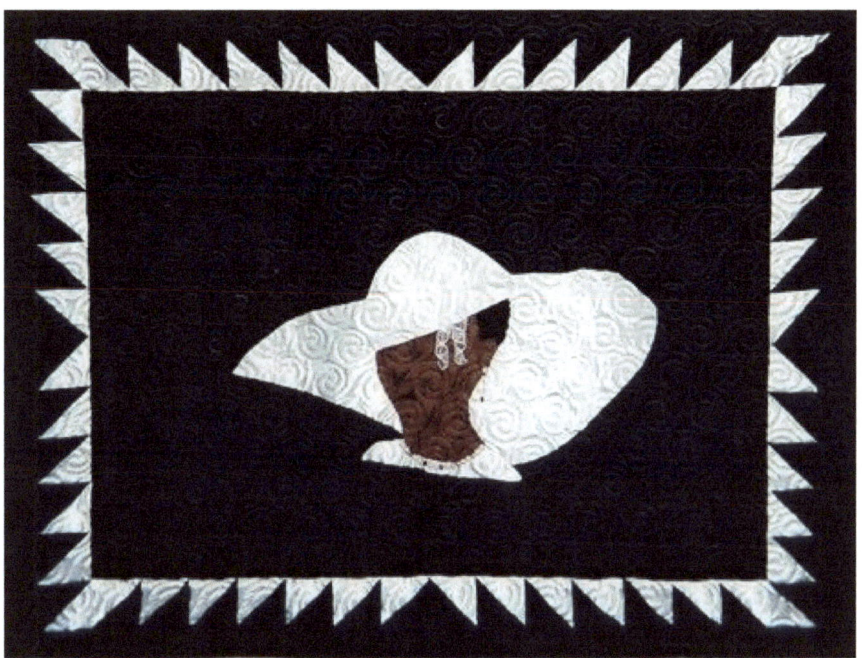

"Mrs. Big 7"
48" x 33"

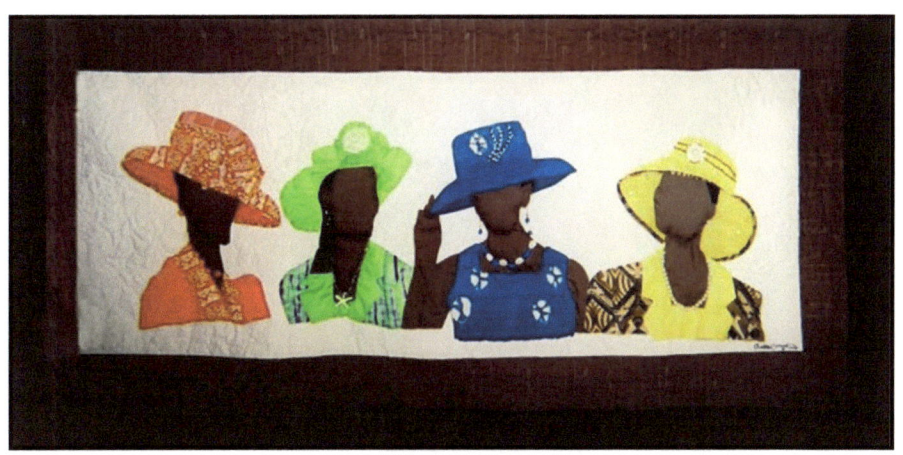

"Sister Love"
58" x 32"

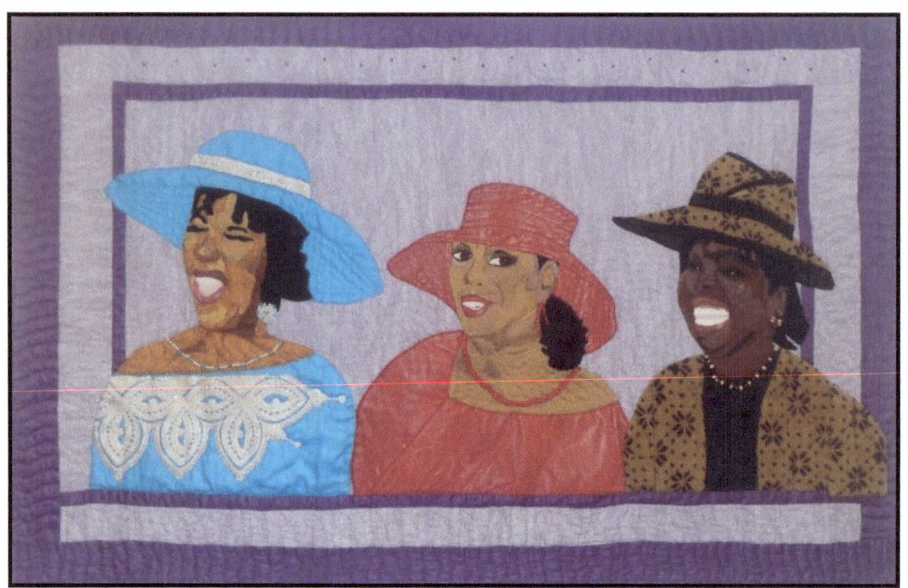

"The Conversation"
56" x 36"

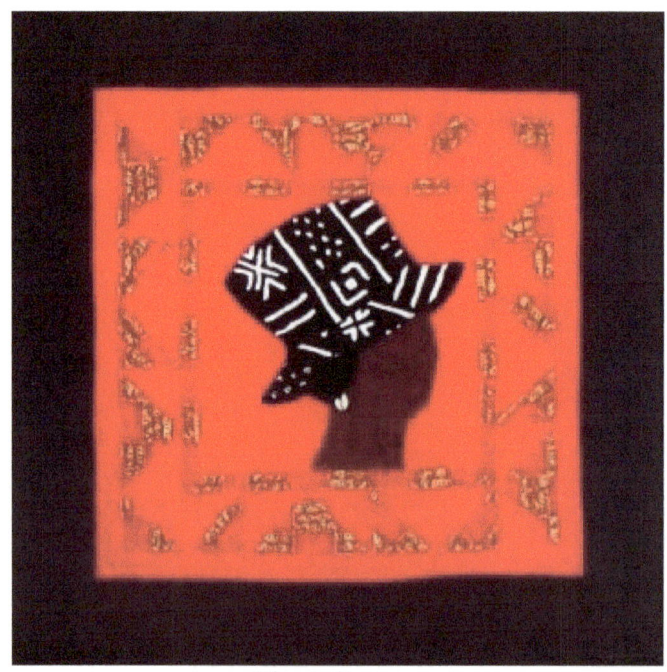

"Josie"
35" x 35"

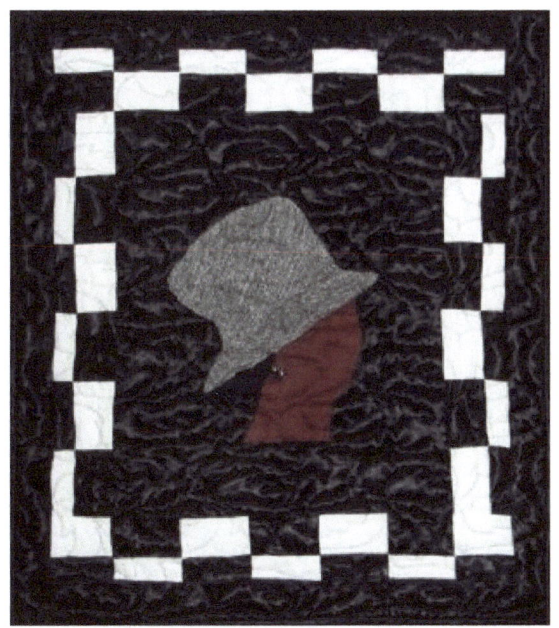

"Josie 2"
31" x 36"

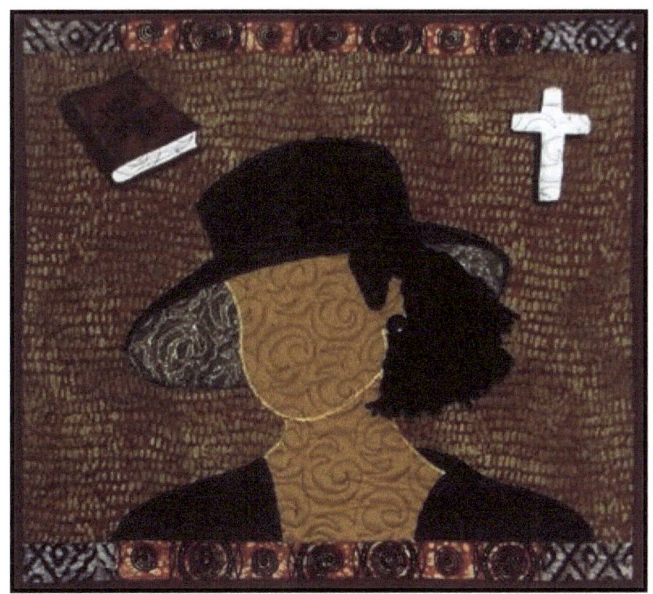

"Vendya"
22" x 28"

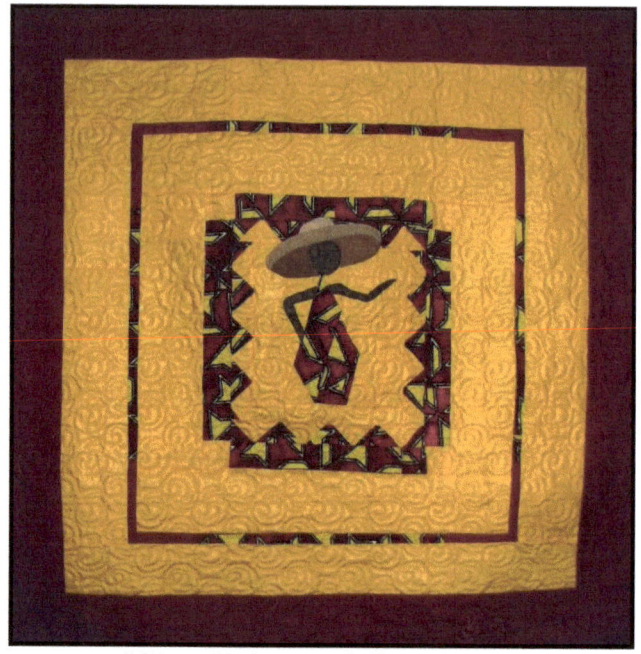

"Simplicity and Sunshine"
39" x 39"

I first started making the Mrs. Big Series. I loved creating the BIG hat. There was a woman in my home town that wore a really big hat like that to church. Everyone whispered about her because her husband was "Mr. Big". You know Mr. Big is the big shot guy in town that does a few unscrupulous things, gets away with it and has a beautiful wife. She flaunts her beauty and brandishes a BIG hat.

Next I was commissioned to create Sister Love for a lovely woman in Texas that had three sisters. She wanted to honor their friendship in a quilt. I didn't know them personally but wanted to create a quilt that showed four different personalities as I was sure they all displayed. She absolutely loved it.

The Conversation was one of my early portrait quilts. I was commissioned to make a quilt with three women. I was already on a roll making women with hats so I thought I would make hats as well as faces. As I worked on The Conversation, I felt as though they were at an affair having a discreet conversation among themselves.

I was asked to make a quilt with a bible and a cross and my cousin Vendya Little died around the same time. I named the quilt after her as my tribute to one of the cousins that influenced my life.

I tried a lot of hat styles and really liked making the hat quilts. Willow became a tribute to my mother-in-law, Willow Cochran. Josie was a tribute to my grandmother, Josephine Crockett Lewis. The hat I used on Josie reminded me of one she would have worn.

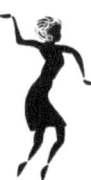

4

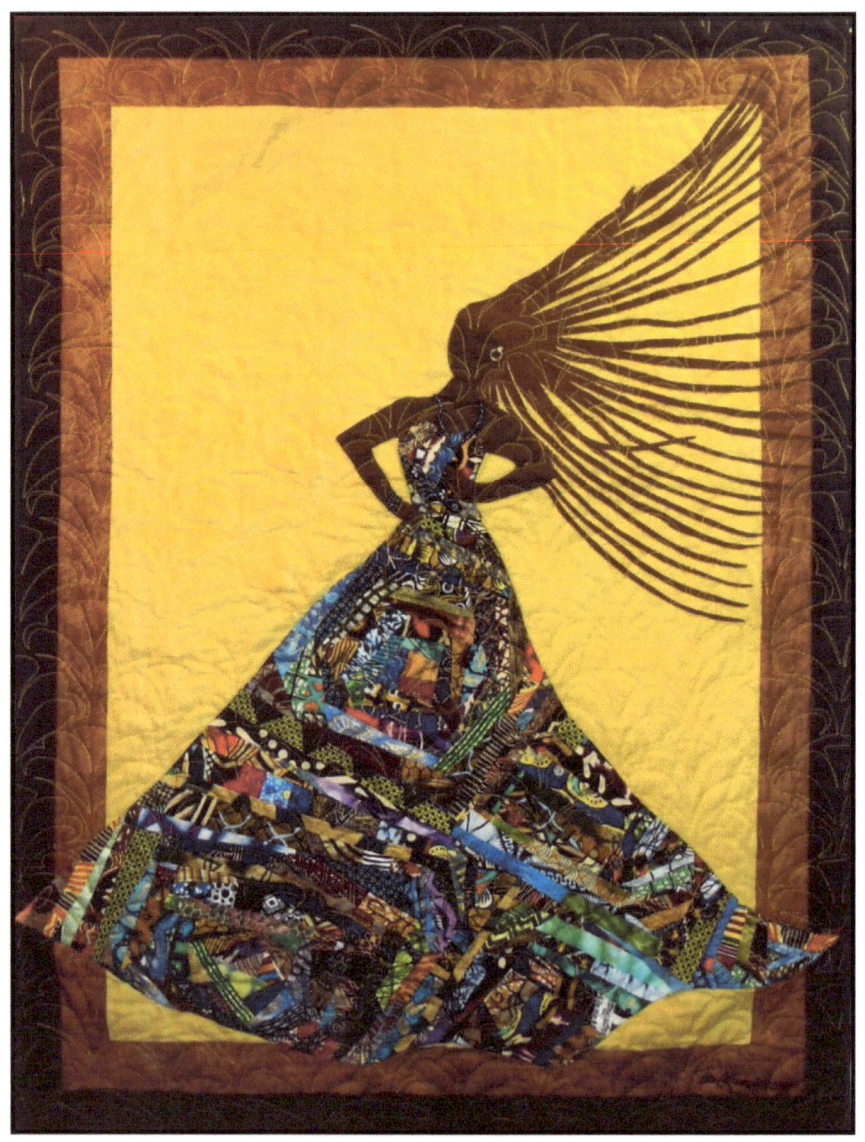

SHE IS
THE HAIR REVOLUTION

These quilts were inspired by the idea that hair is not the total sum of ones worth. The idea that we may one day live in a society where we are not judged by the length and straightness of our hair.

I was awakened to the beauty of my own natural hair in the 1960's. The Black Power Movement of the 60's and early 70's opened our eyes to a new view of our African heritage. It was the beginning of learning to "love ourselves"; the way we look, the natural curl of our hair, the color of our skin and the speech pattern we adopted over centuries. I call this new idea of wearing natural hair- The Hair Revolution.

The dress is made of a myriad of scrap fabrics. This quilt features many creative techniques such as appliqué, fabric piecing and beaded embellishments. Many variations of this quilt exist from students who have taken my workshop or read my book- "Scrap Easy: Building a Collage Quilt". I am so pleased to see their innovative results.

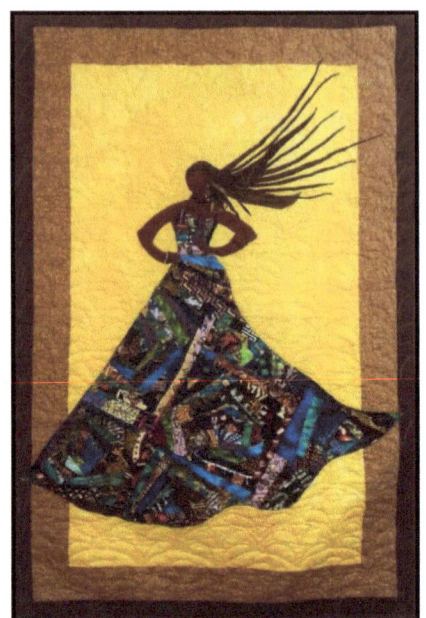

"I Am Not My Hair"
47" x 52"

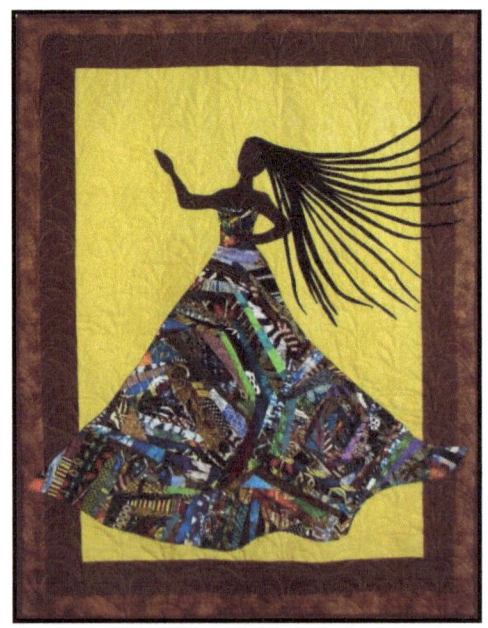

"I Am Not My Hair 2"
44" x 50"

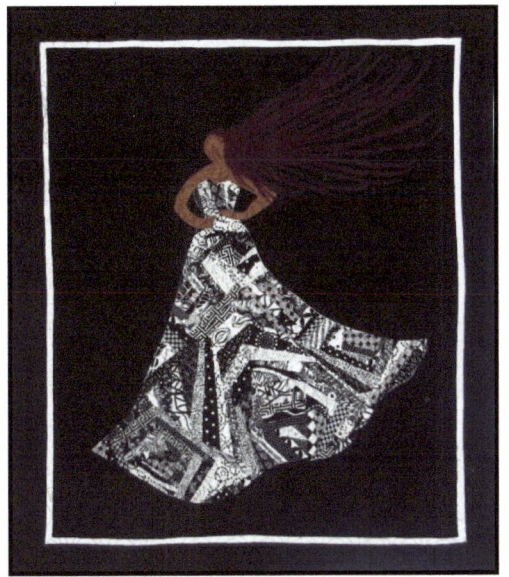

"I Am Not My Hair 3"
44" x 50"

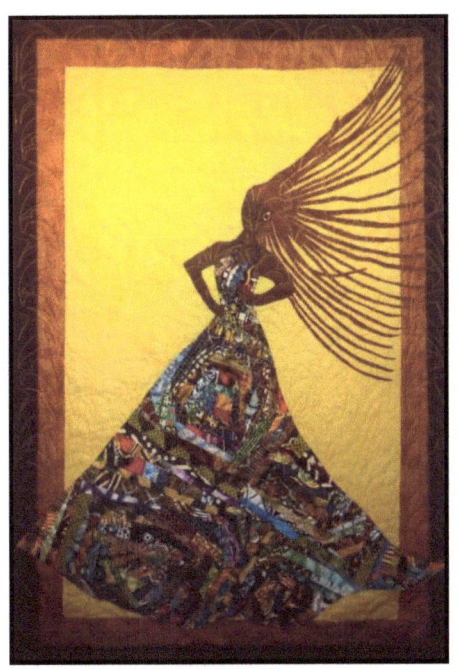

"I Am Not My Hair 4"
48" x 55"

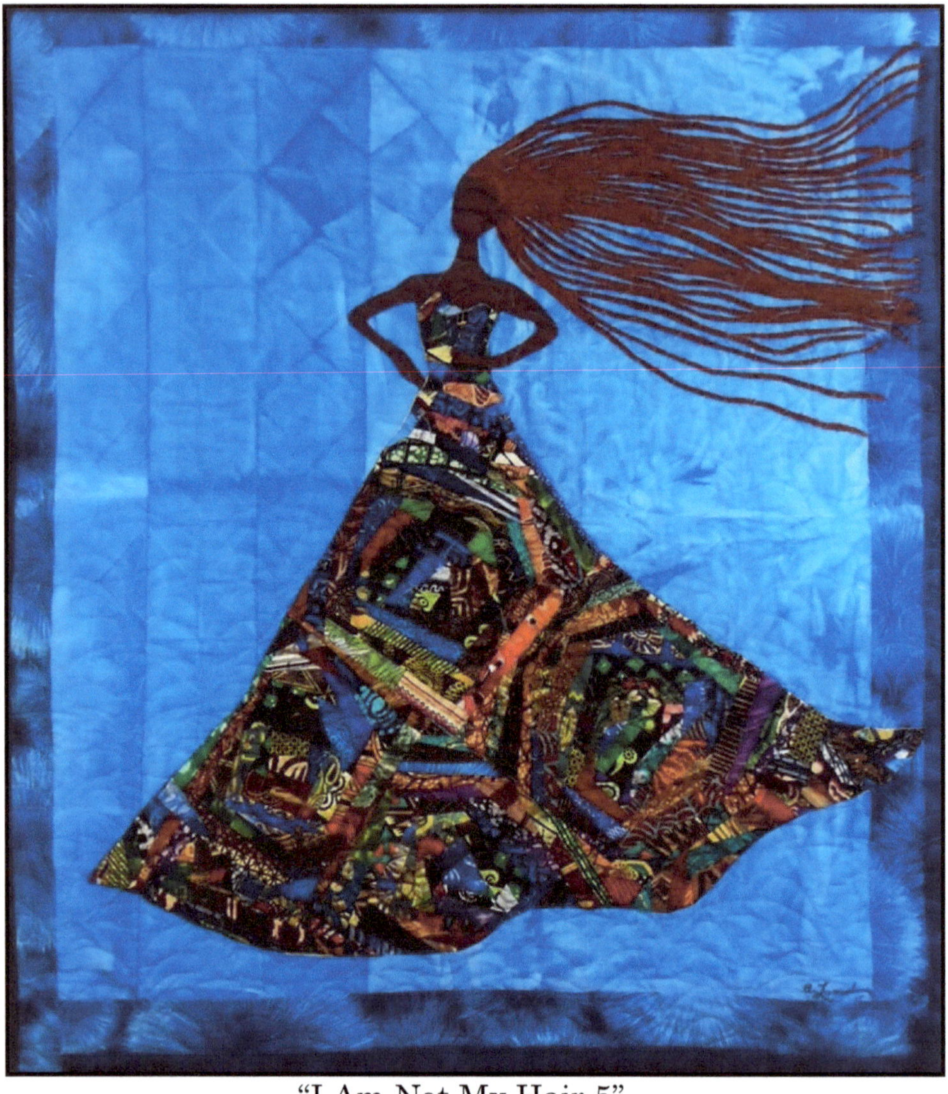

"I Am Not My Hair 5"
41" x 46"

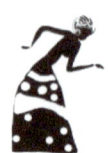

5

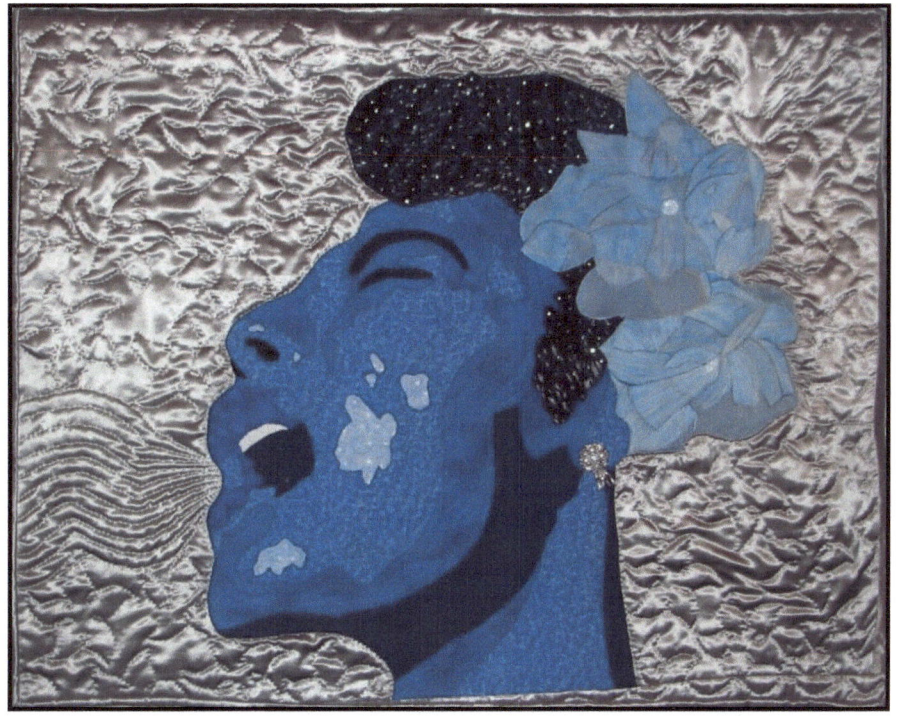

SHE IS LEGENDARY

These quilts were inspired by the idea that a portrait could be created with fabric and be just as beautiful as the paint media.

As I thumbed through a quilt magazine, I saw a quilt with a picture of a man with a little boy on it. I was inspired to create a face on a quilt similar to that one. Later (after I had made Sidney Poitier), I found out that the faces I had admired so much in that magazine were painted on and then quilted. It didn't matter because I liked what I was doing with piecing.

I spent a great amount of time developing my technique for bringing photographs to fiber art. Social media introduced me to other great quilt artists who had been doing portrait quilts and many more quilt artists that have since joined the ranks. Each time I make a portrait quilt my technique improves.

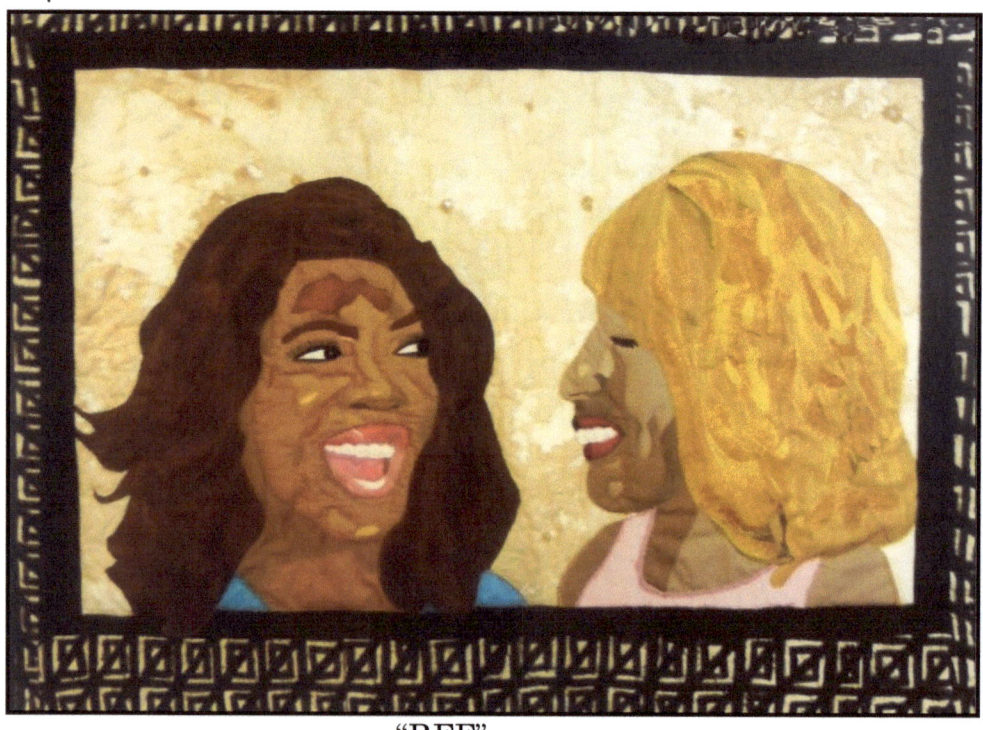

"BFF"
50" x 38"
Oprah Winfrey and Gayle King

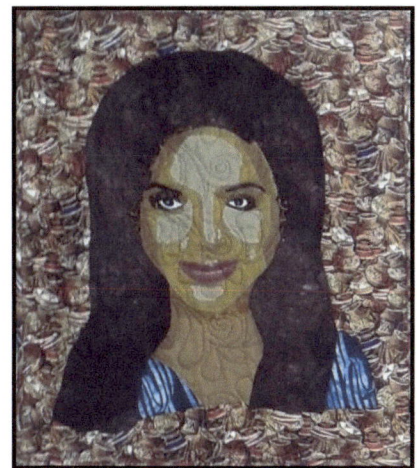

"Claire"
23" x 28"
Felicia Rashad

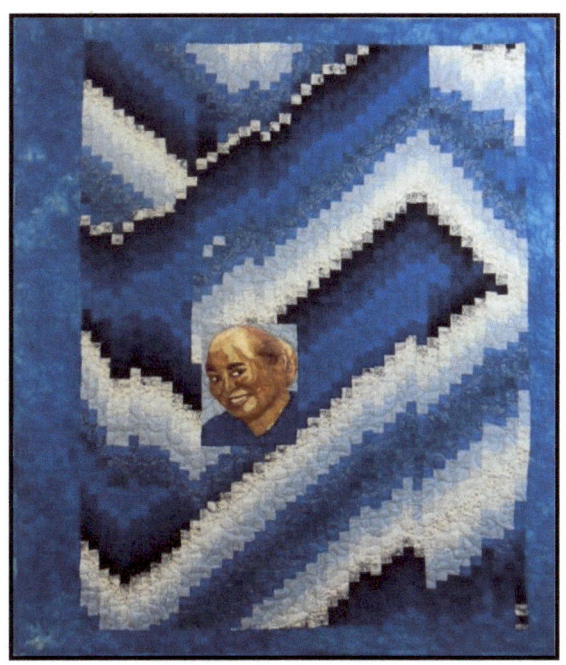

"First In Line"
44" x 54"
Hattie McDaniel

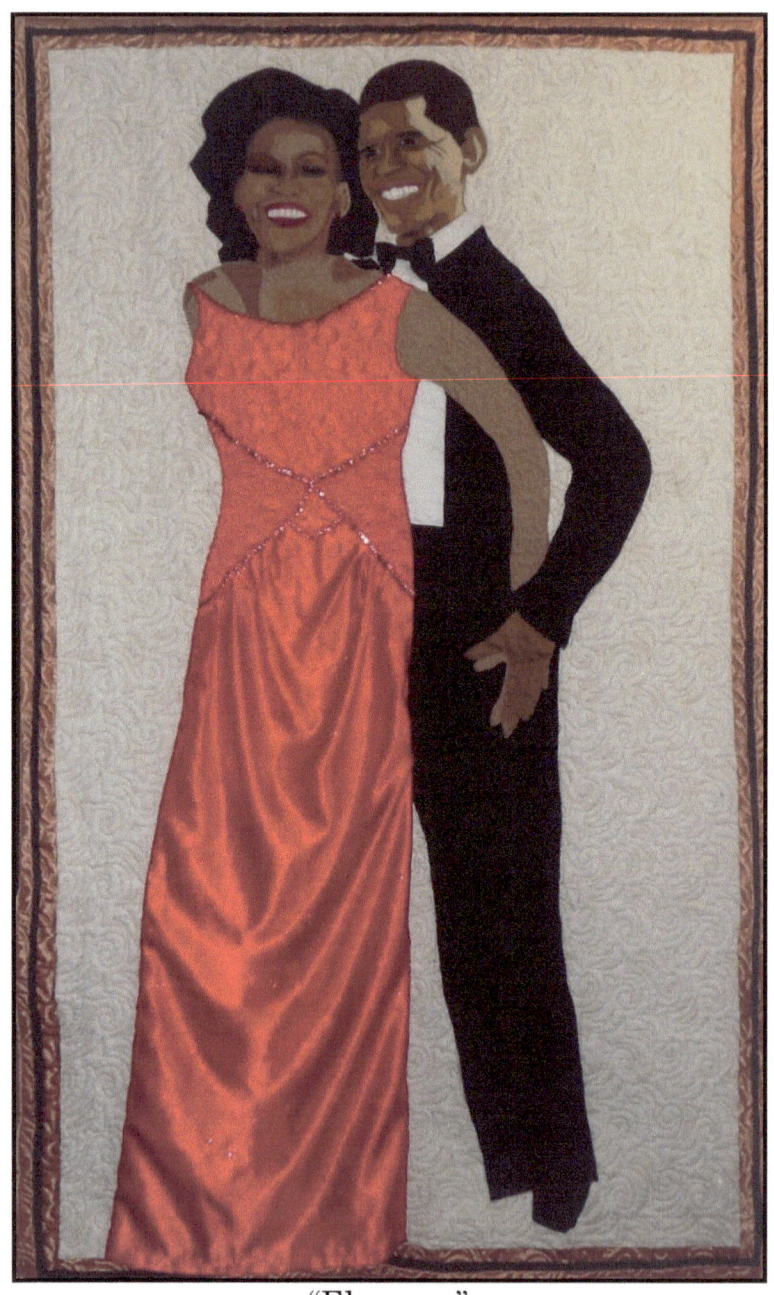

"Elegance"
46" x 76"
First Lady Michelle Obama

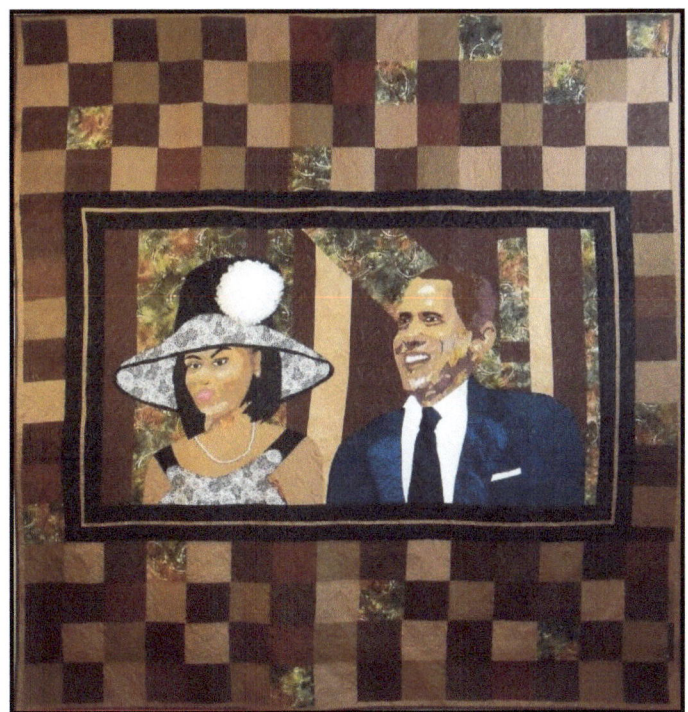

Just Between Us
95" x 98"
First Lady Michelle Obama

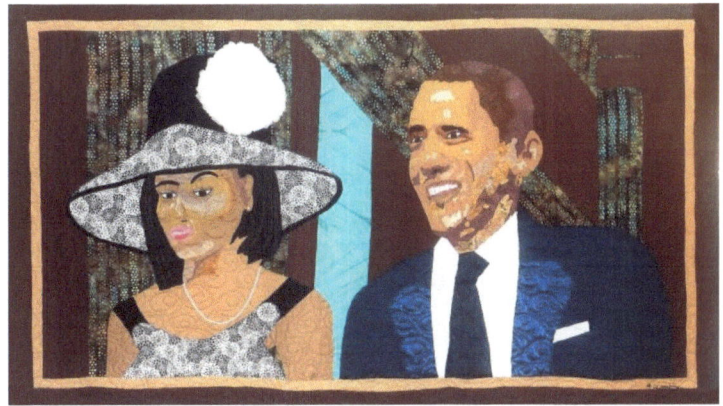

Just Between Us 2
71" x 42"
First Lady Michelle Obama

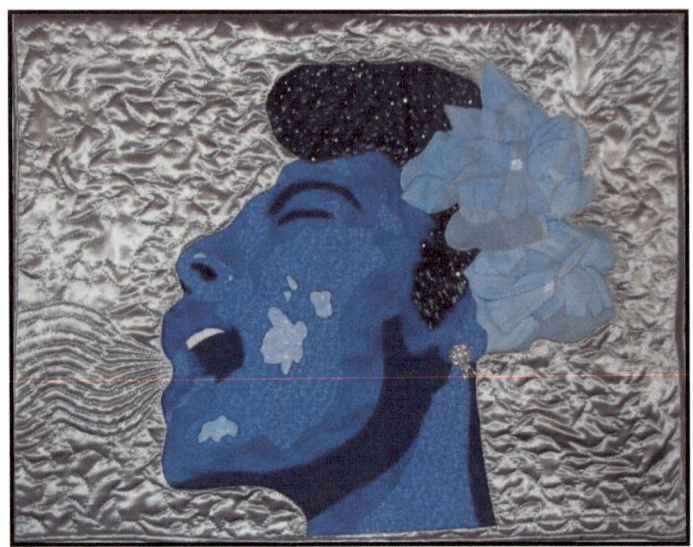

"Lady Sings"
48" x 39"
Billie Holiday

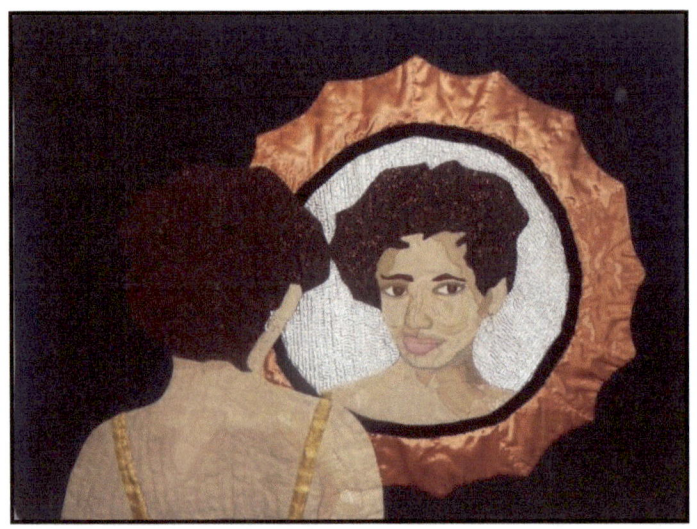

"Leading Lady"
50" x 38"
Halle Berry

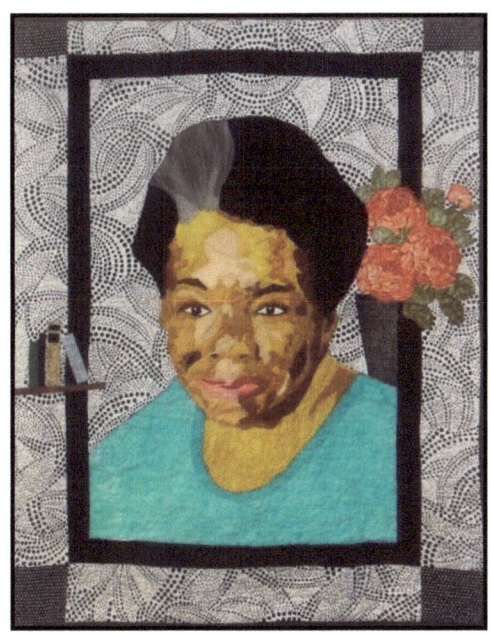

"Maya Speaks Truth"
36" x 49"
Maya Angelou

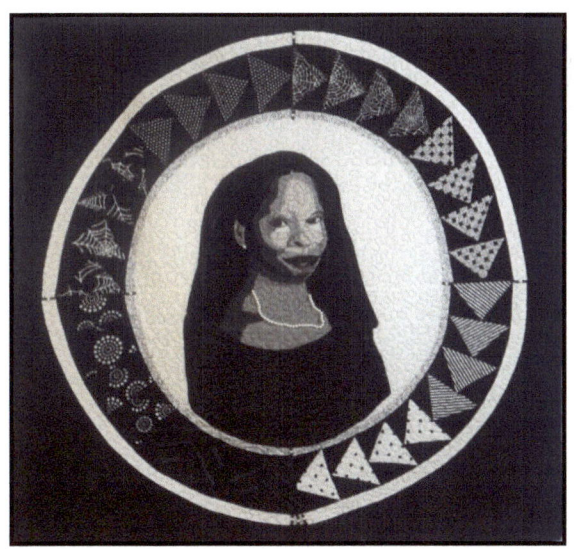

"My Own Terms"
42" x 41"
Whoopi Goldberg

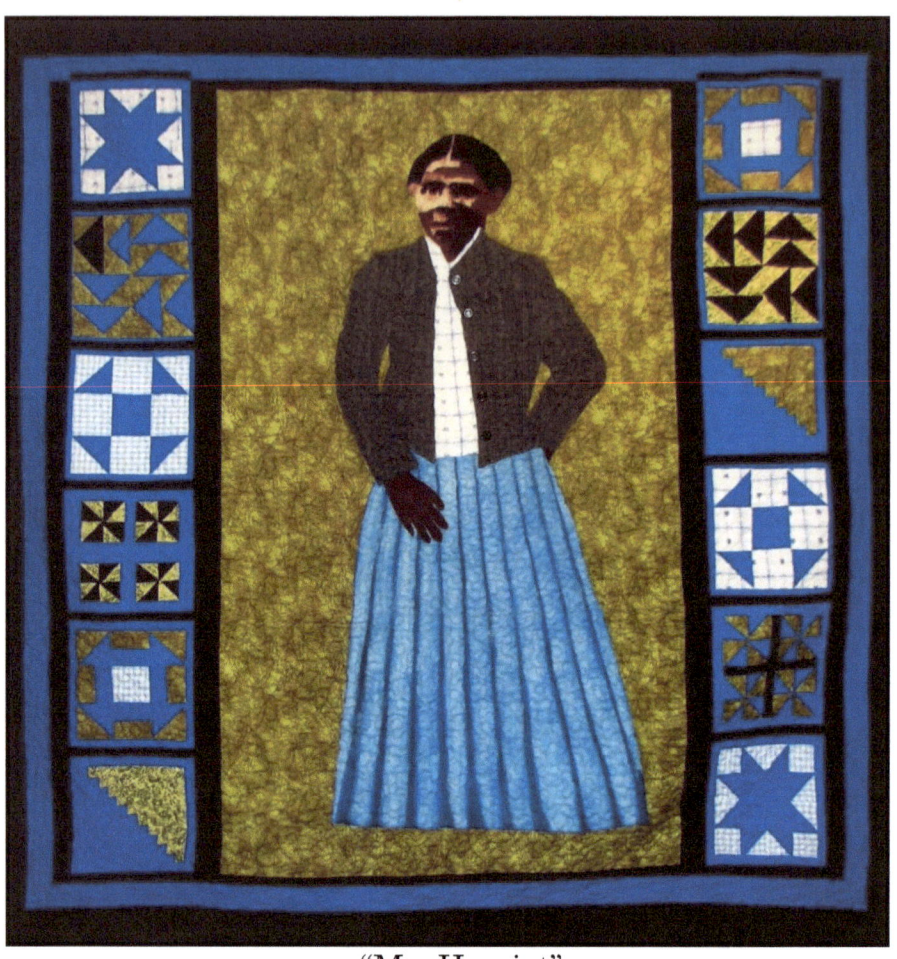

"Ms. Harriet"
82" X 94"
Harriet Tubman

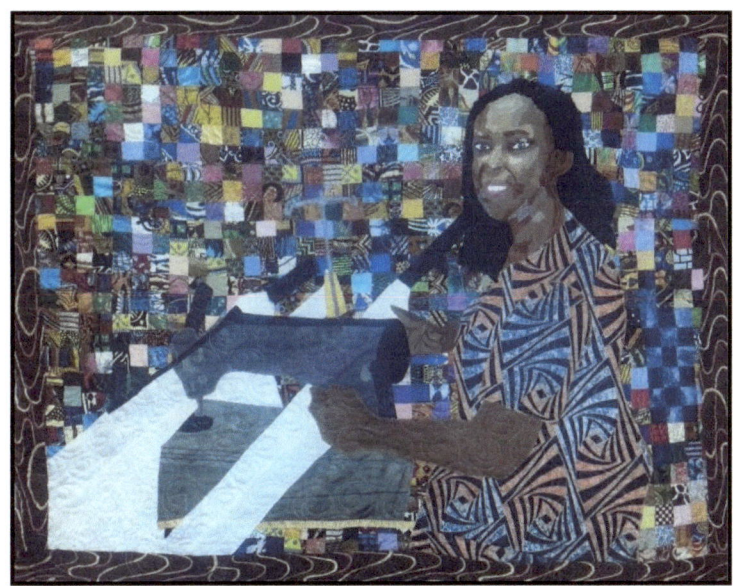

"My Passion My Peace"
56" x 44"
Aisha Lumumba

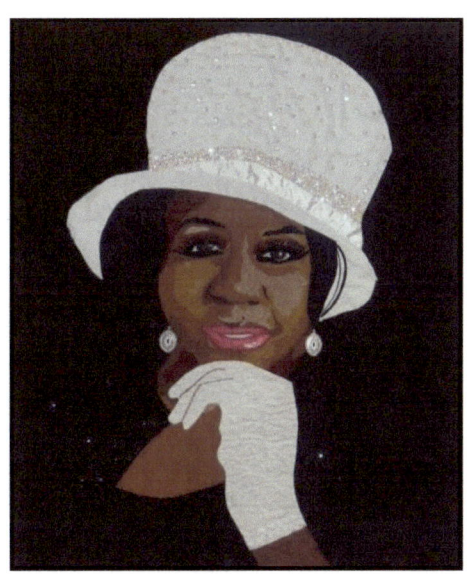

"R.E.S.P.E.C.T."
34" x 44"
Aretha Franklin

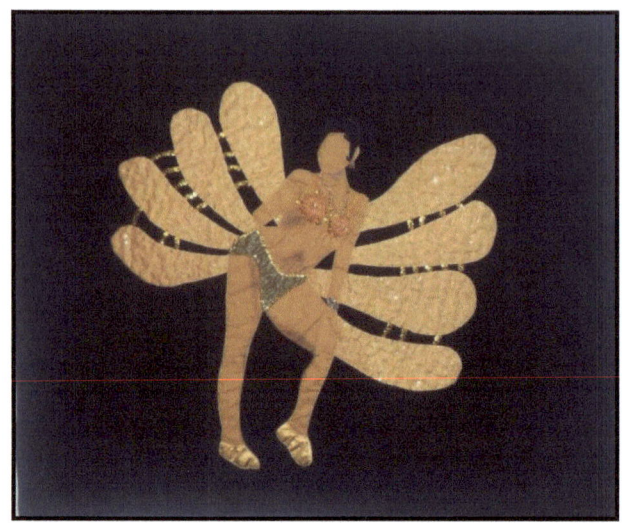

Stunning
43" x 38"
Josephine Baker

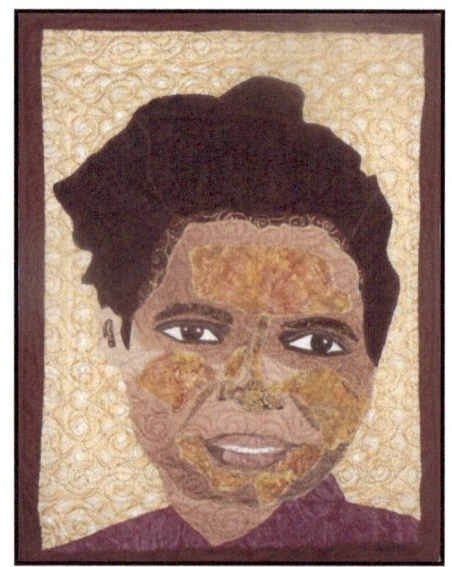

"Taking A Stand"
33" X 35"
Rosa Parks

6

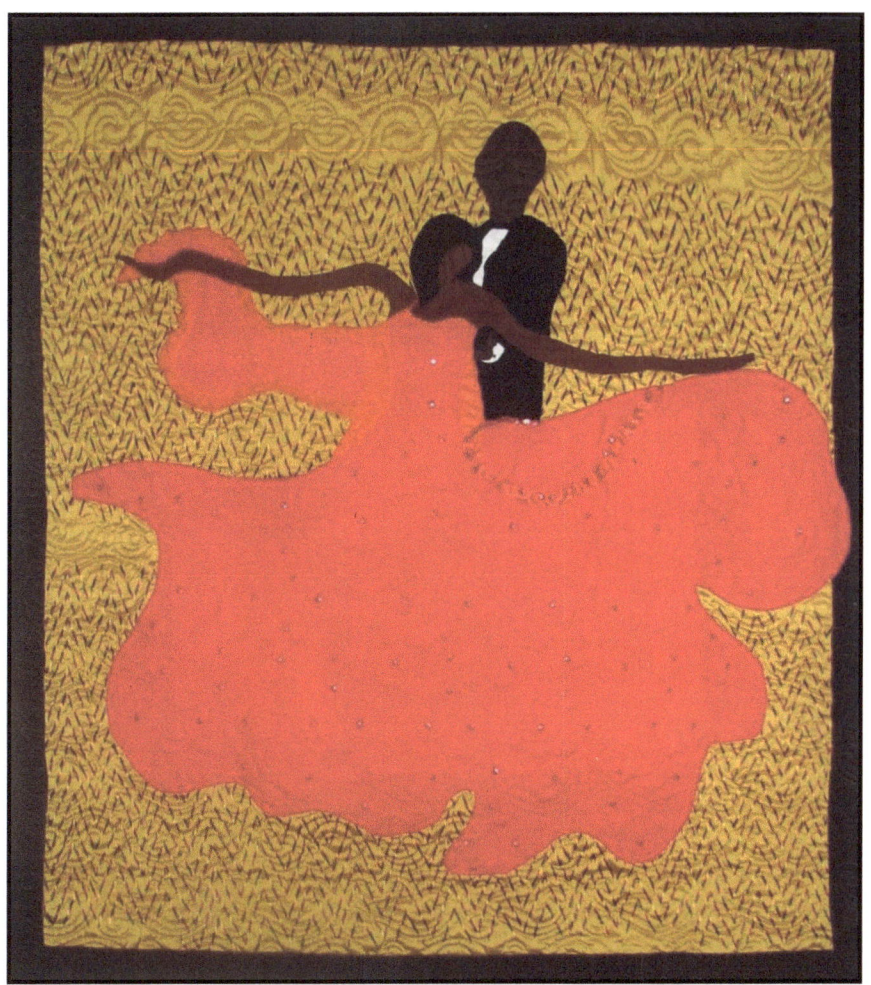

SHE IS DANCE

These quilts are a tribute to dance. Dance is an art form of human performance. It has the ability to enhance and heal your life and being.

Dance was introduced to me when I was very young. I have fond memories of dancing around our living room with my sisters and brothers. Everyone would laugh as I did the twist. As I grew older my love for dancing increased. I still love to dance and love making these quilts that emanate the feeling of flowing movement.

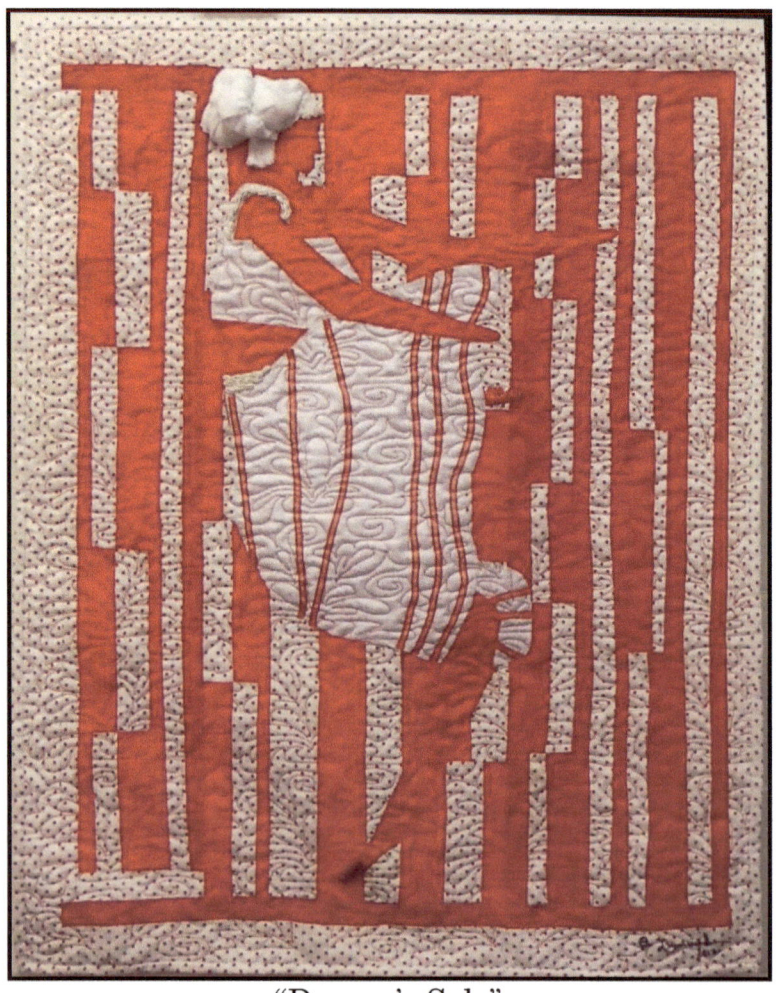

"Dancer's Solo"
37" x 54"

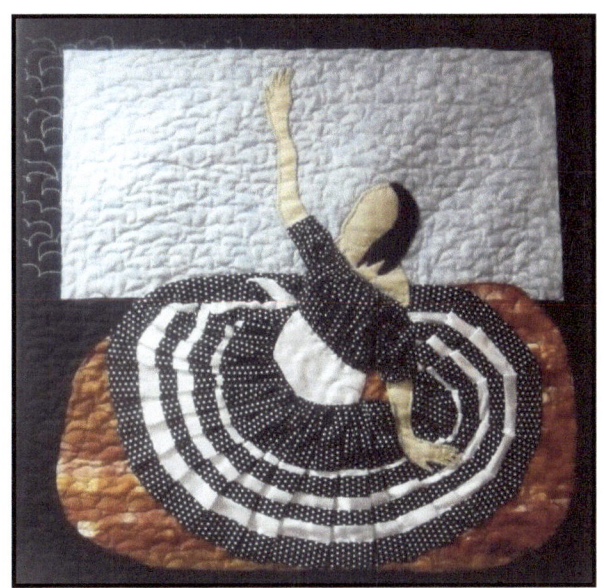

"Dancing Is My Life"
36" x 38"

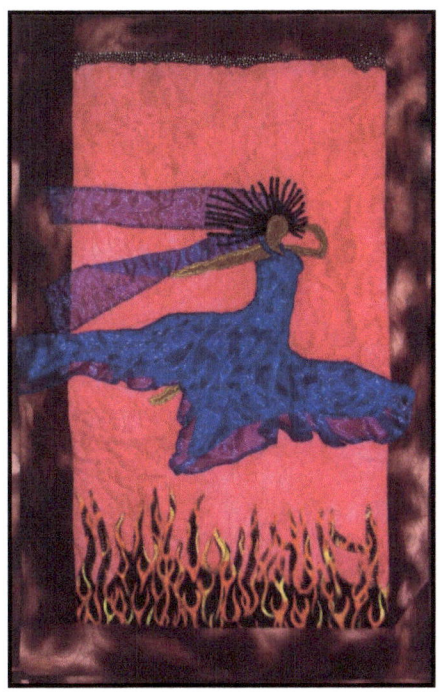

Fire Dancer
18" x 30"

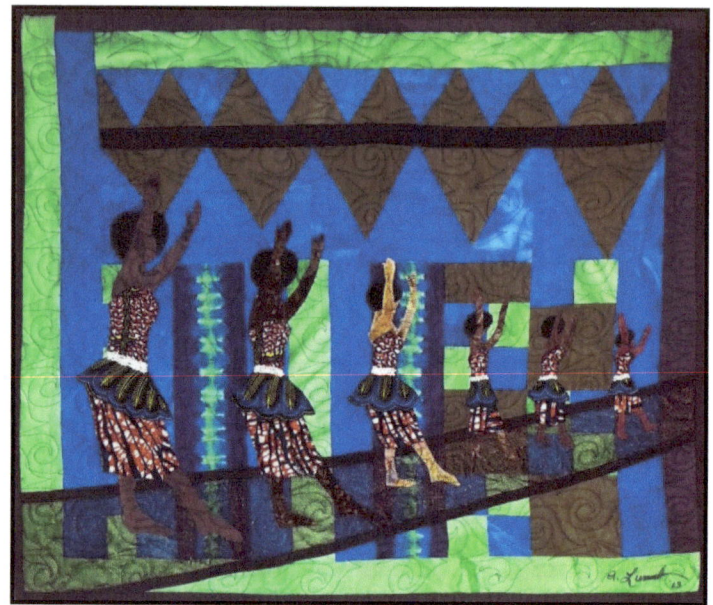

"Funga Alafia: Welcome"
29" x 26"

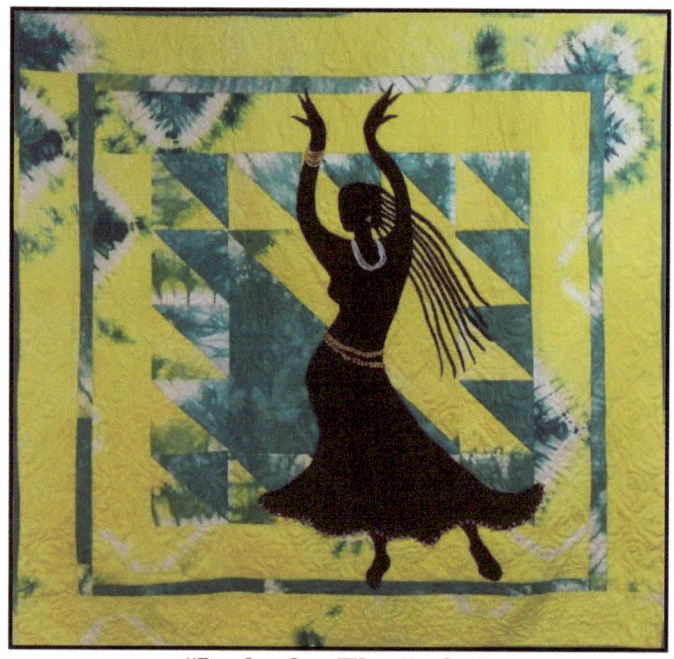

"Lady On The Lake"
48" x 48"

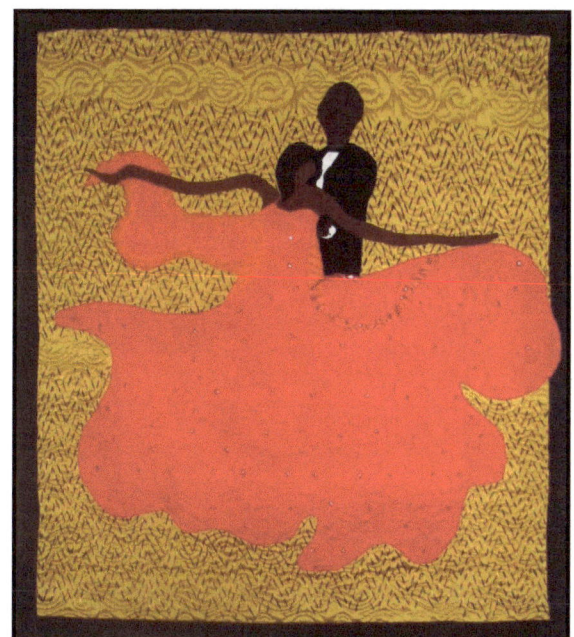

"Rapture in Red"
50" x 65"

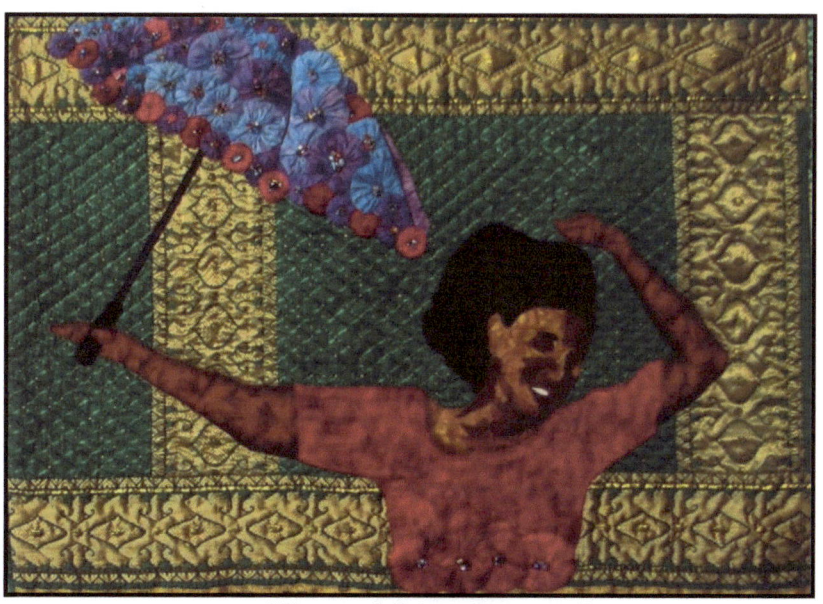

"Second Line Dancer"
45" x 29"

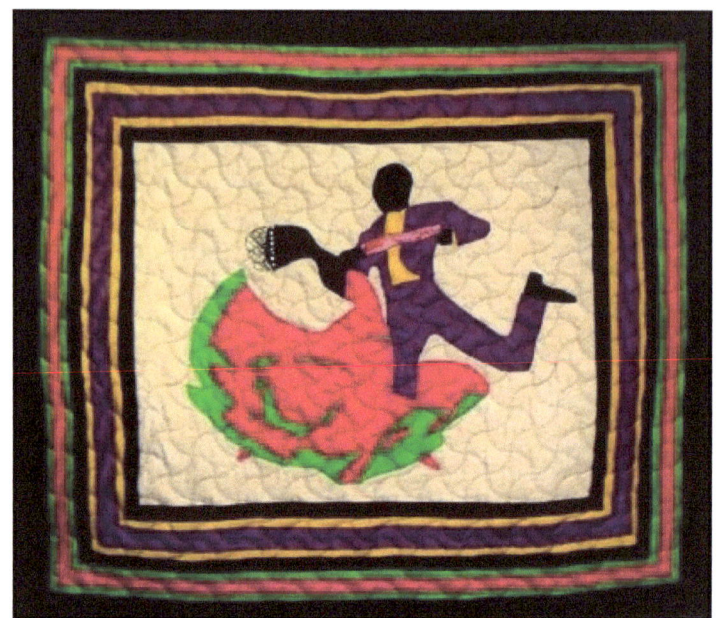

"Swept Away"
41" x 36"

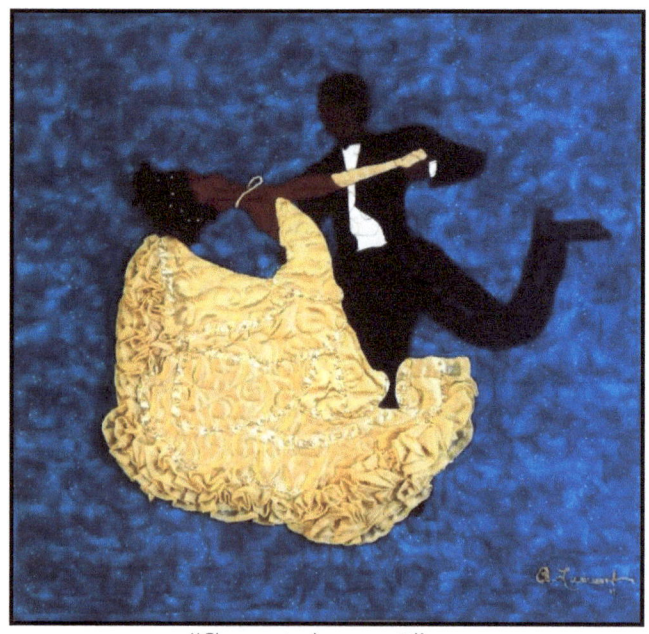

"Swept Away 2"
27" x 26"

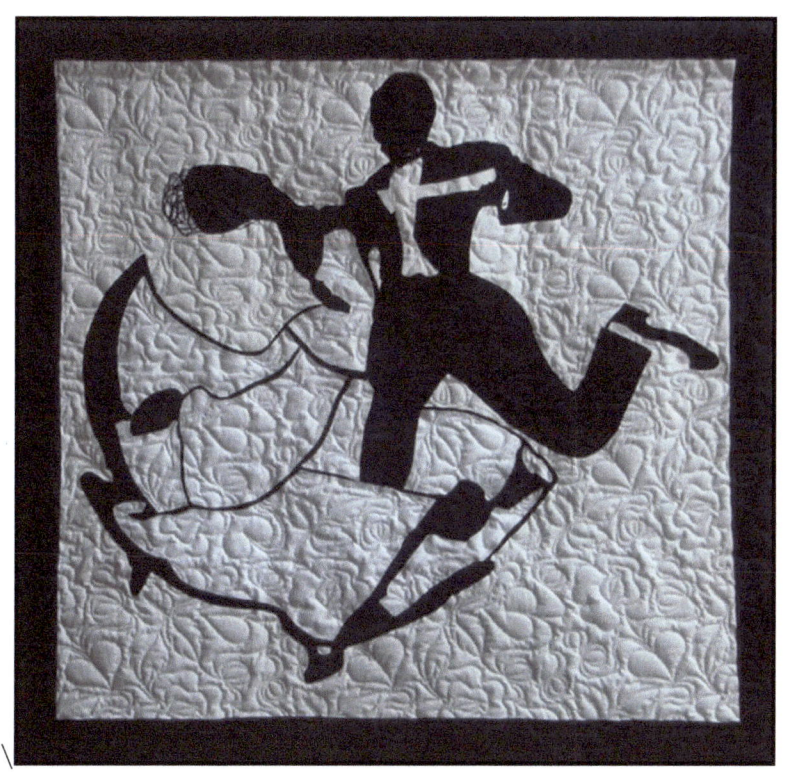

"Two Step"
52" x 64"

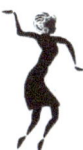

7

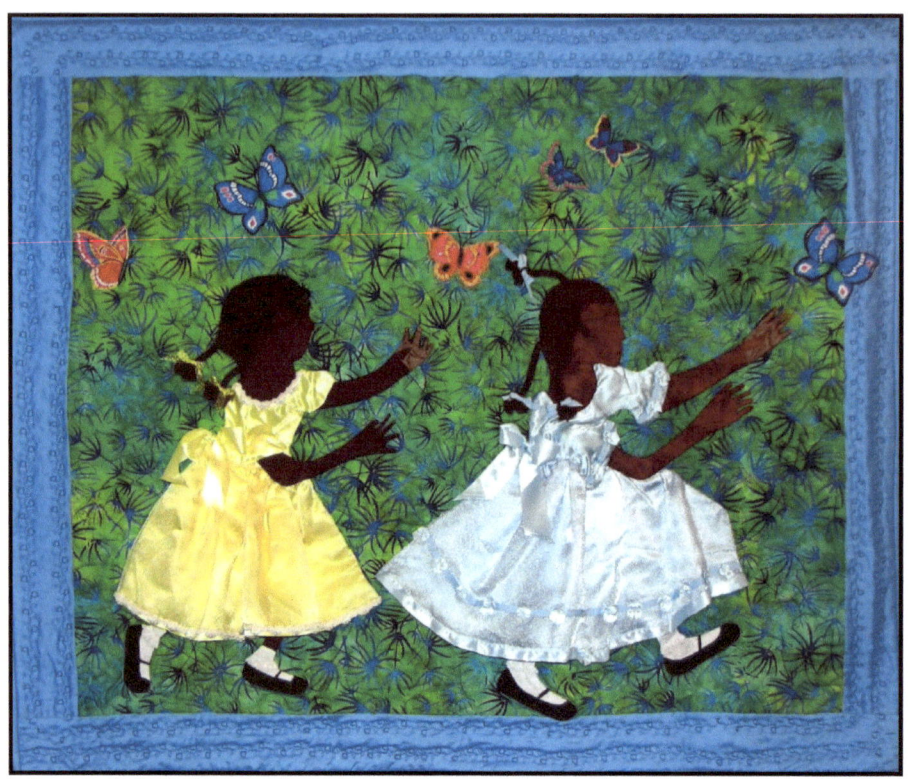

SHE IS GROWING

These quilts are a tribute to siblings and friends everywhere. I have glorious memories of my sisters and my friends. We enjoyed the short time we spent growing up. These quilts take me back to memories of those happy times.

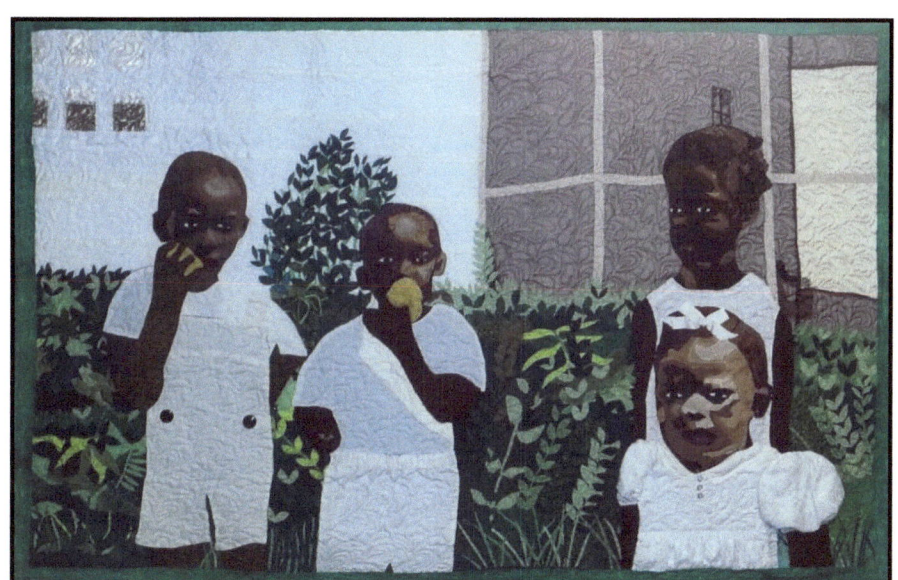

"After The Funeral-1943"
77" x 42"

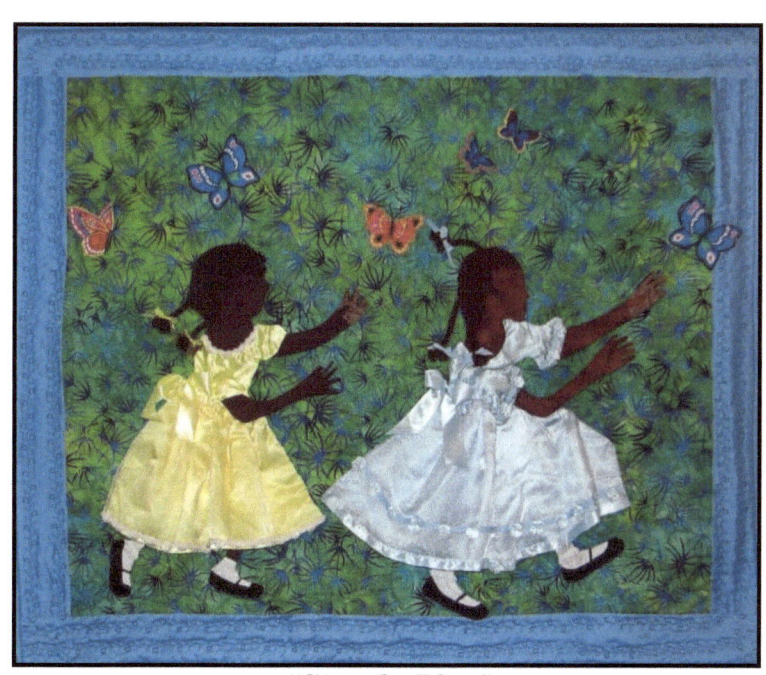

"Simple Play"
50" x 43"

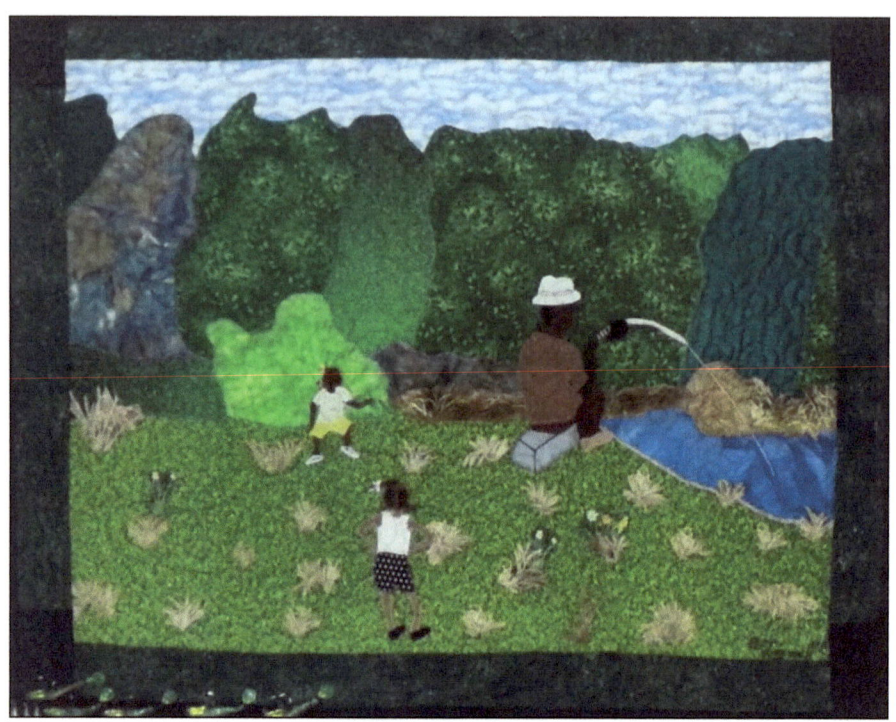

"Fishing With Dad"
41" x 32"

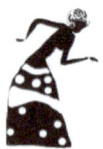

8

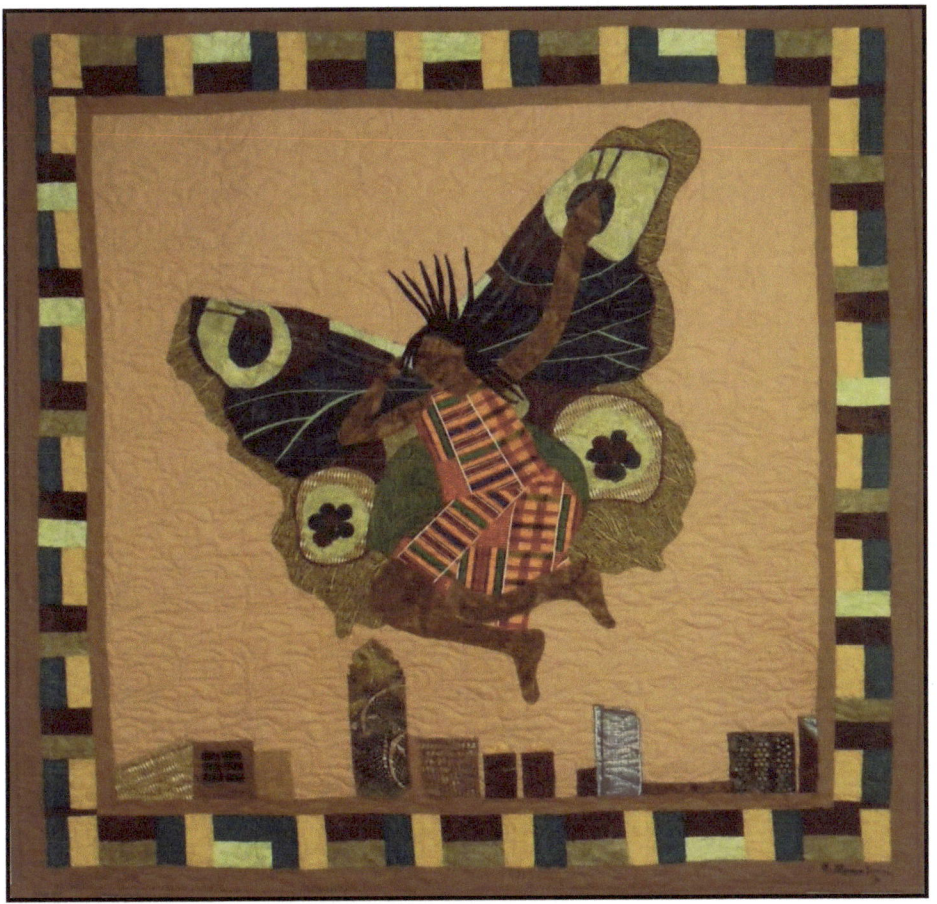

SHE HAS WINGS

These quilts attest to the fact that women fly above turmoil in their lives. The Only Women Have Wings series celebrates women making it despite of the odds working against them on so many levels.

I was totally inspired to make women with wings after studying butterflies when preparing for our exhibit called Metamorphosis. The idea of wings and soaring high above intrigued me.

The ancient Kamitian (Egyptian) people placed bird heads on depictions of people to indicate the ability to soar above earthly pursuits and trials. The Christian religion attribute wings to spirit beings called Angels to show the rewards a faithful life will get you in heaven (Afterlife). Some cultures in the United Kingdom consider fairies as magical spirit people with wings. The airplane started from an idea of humans flying.

Either way we look at it, wings on people are a symbol of aspiring to something greater than yourself and higher than your circumstance.

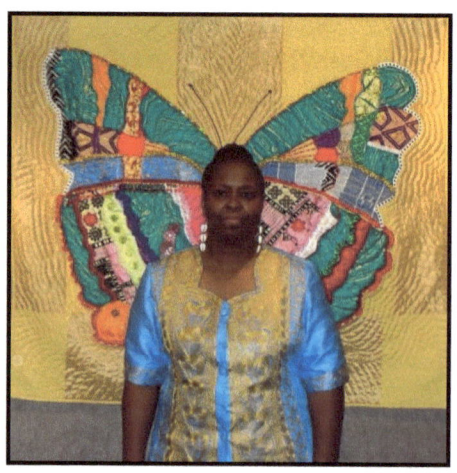

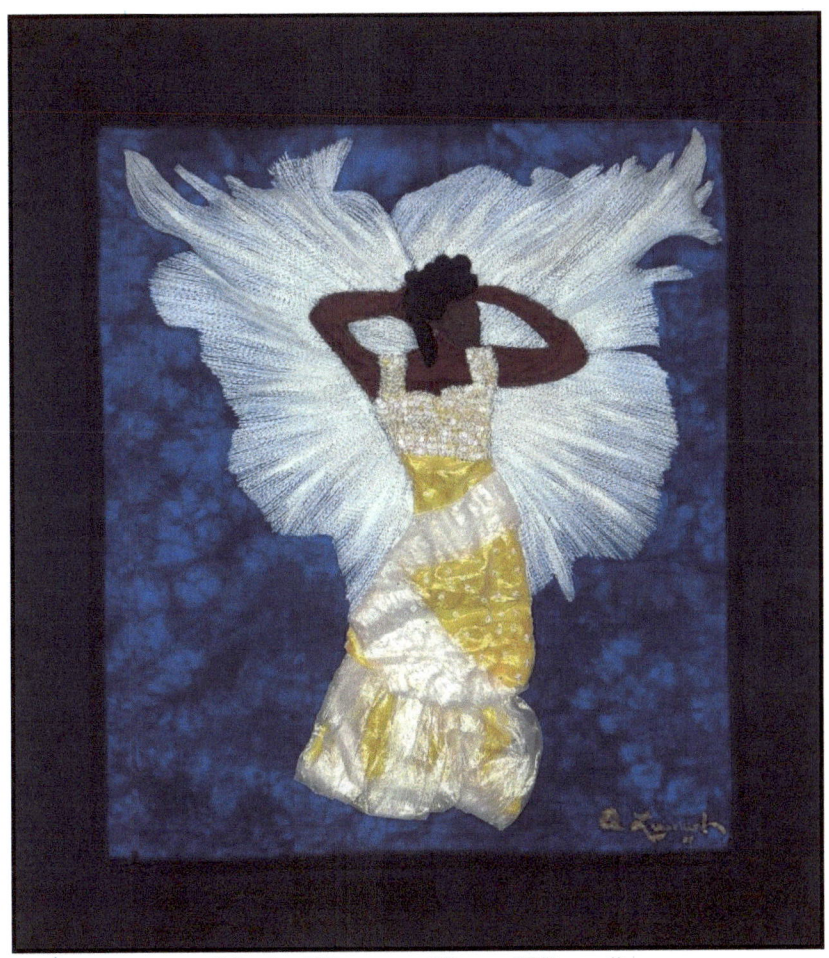

"Only Women Have Wings"
18" x 21"

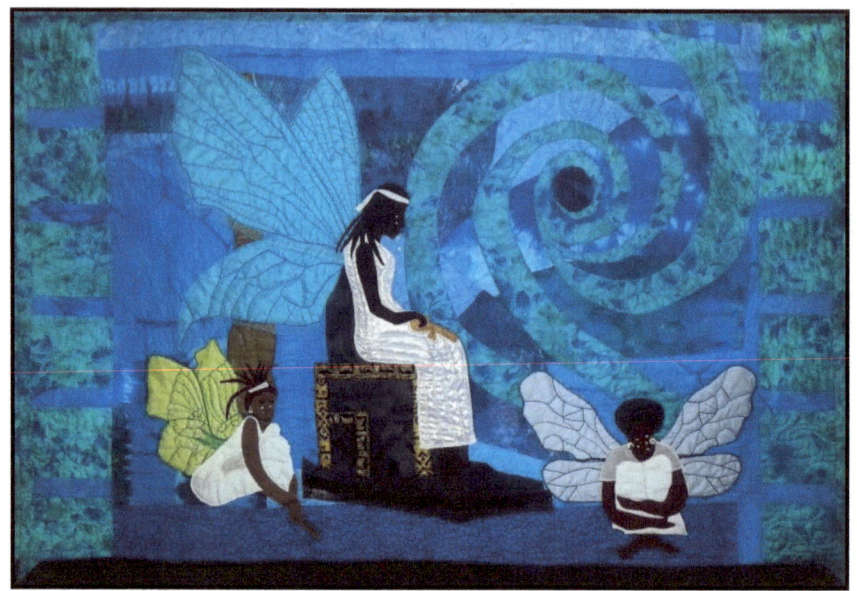

"And The Angels Cried"
60" x 41"

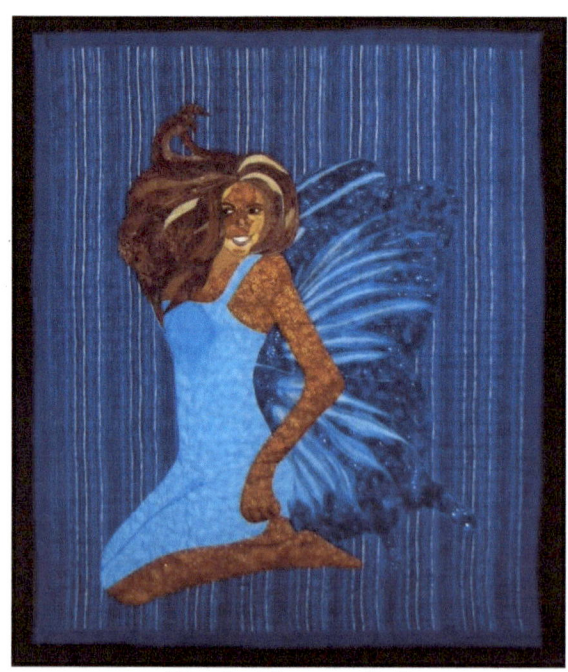

"Lady Butterfly"
50" x 60"

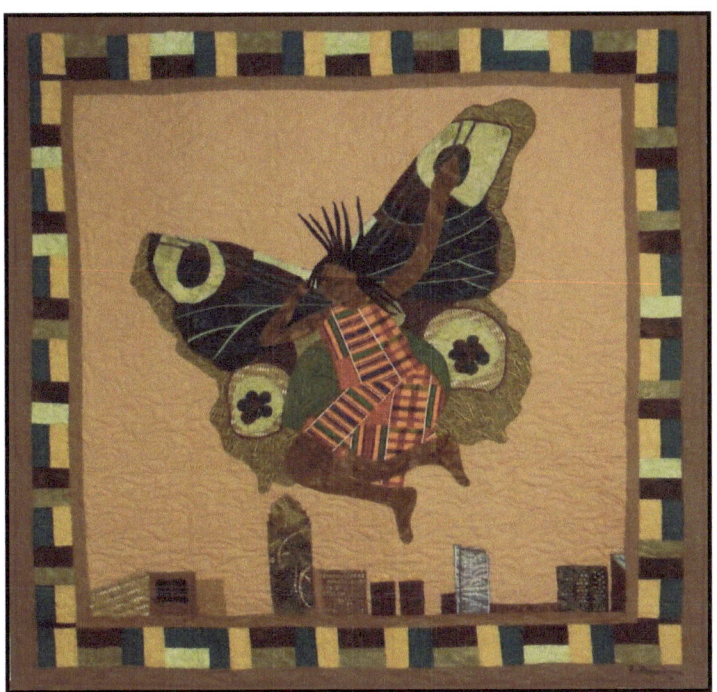

"Only Women Have Wings 2: Leap"
45" x 47"

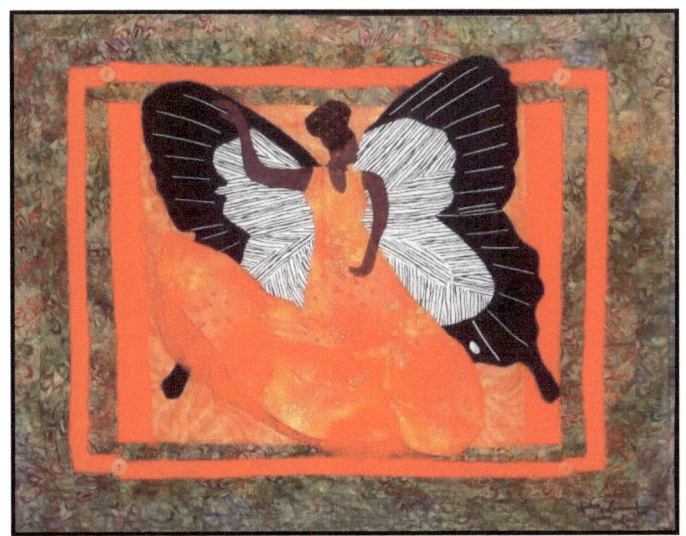

"Only Women Have Wings 3: Love To Dance"
31" x 27"

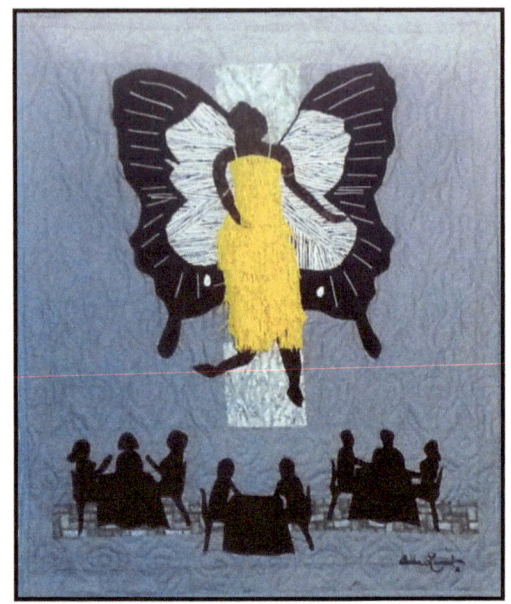

"Only Women Have Wings 4: 1921"
28" x 35"

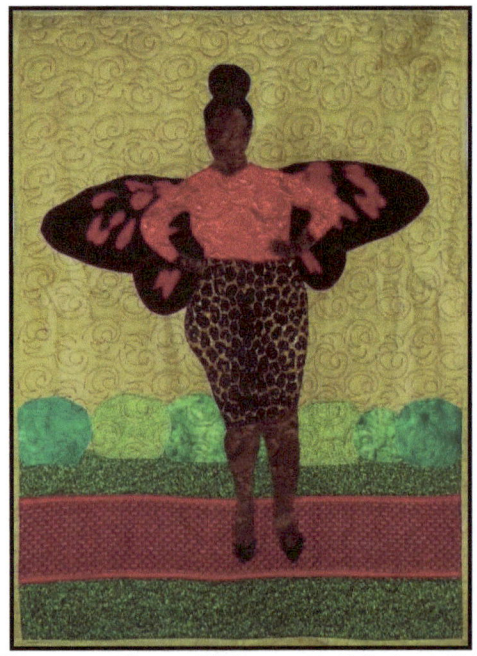

"Only Women Have Wings 5: Wait A Minute "
25.5" x 35"

9

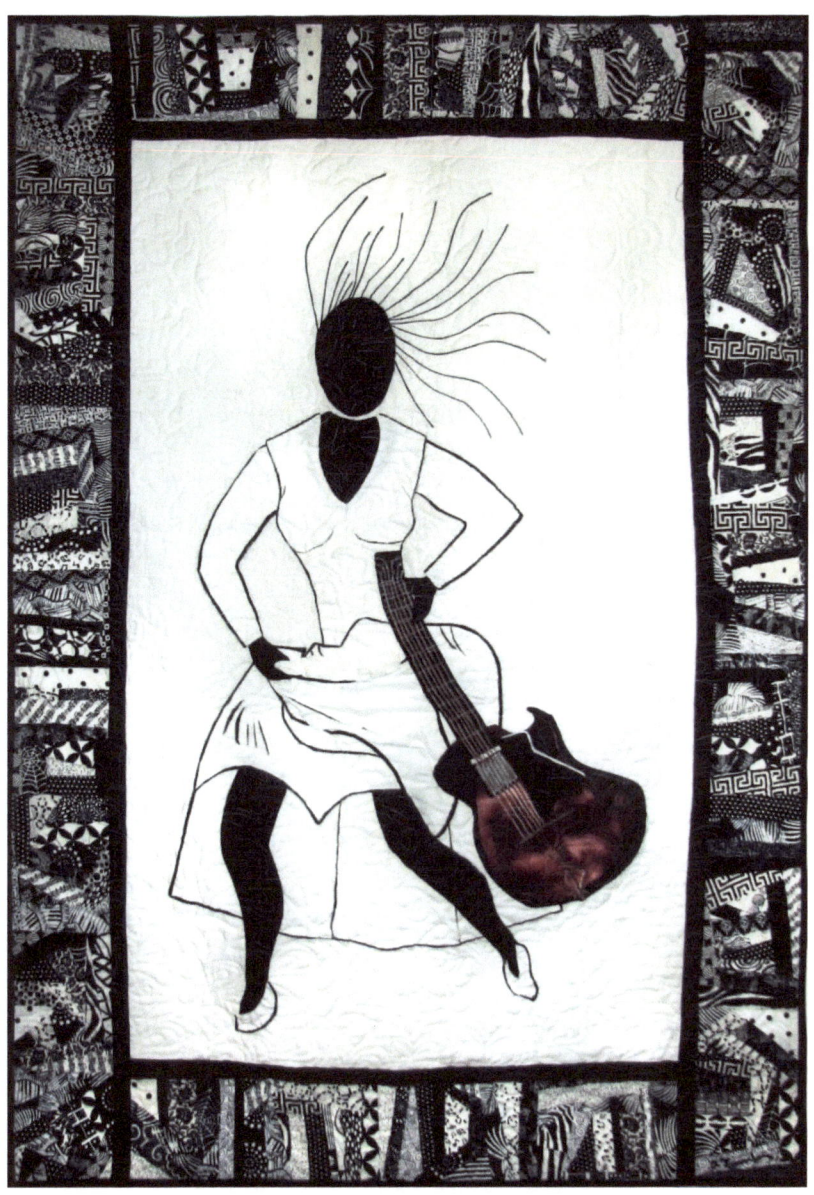

SHE IS A MUSICIAN

These quilts honor women musicians who often become unsung heroes of the music world.

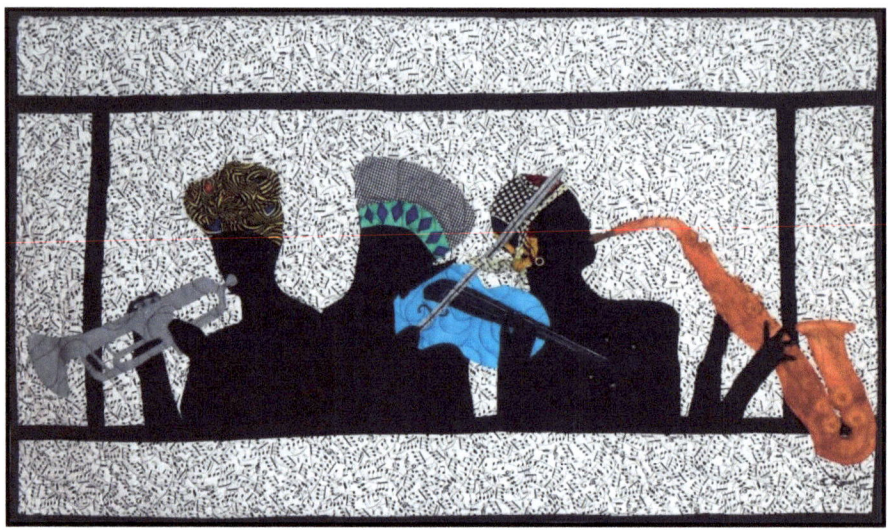

"Jam Session"
46" x 27"

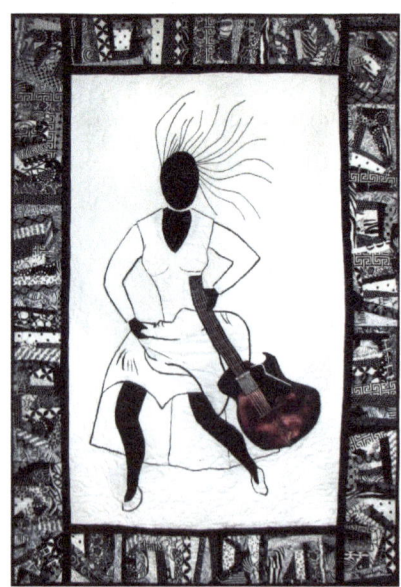

"Running Late"
40" x 61"

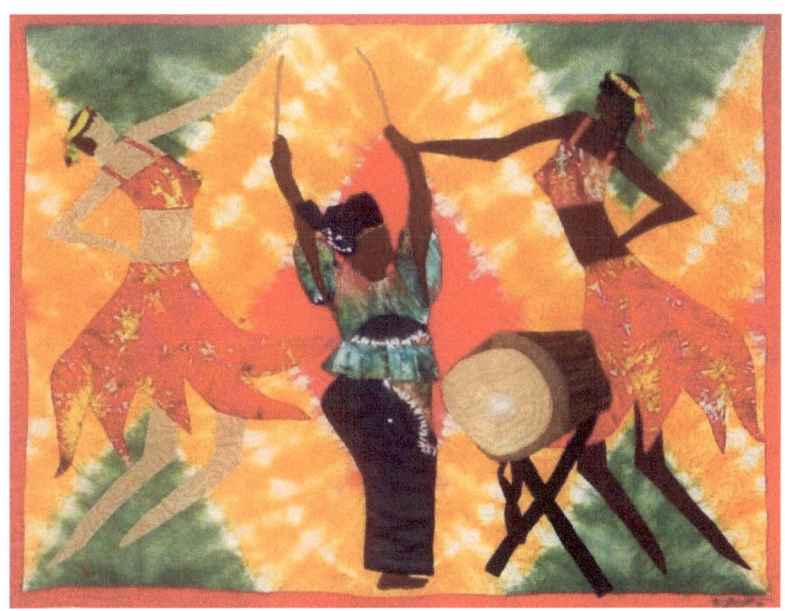

"Rhythms"
38" x 44"

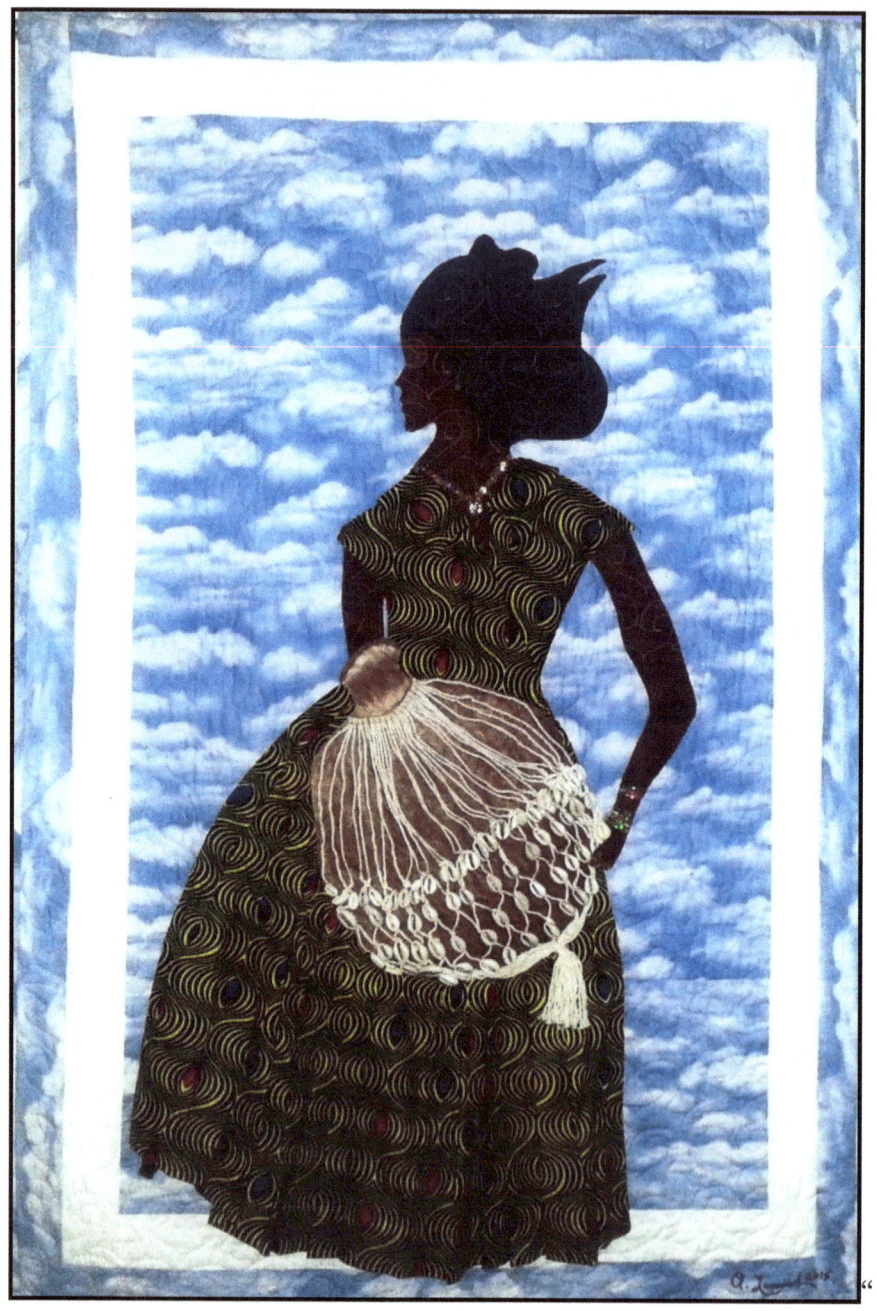

"Mama Shekere"
34" x 51"

10

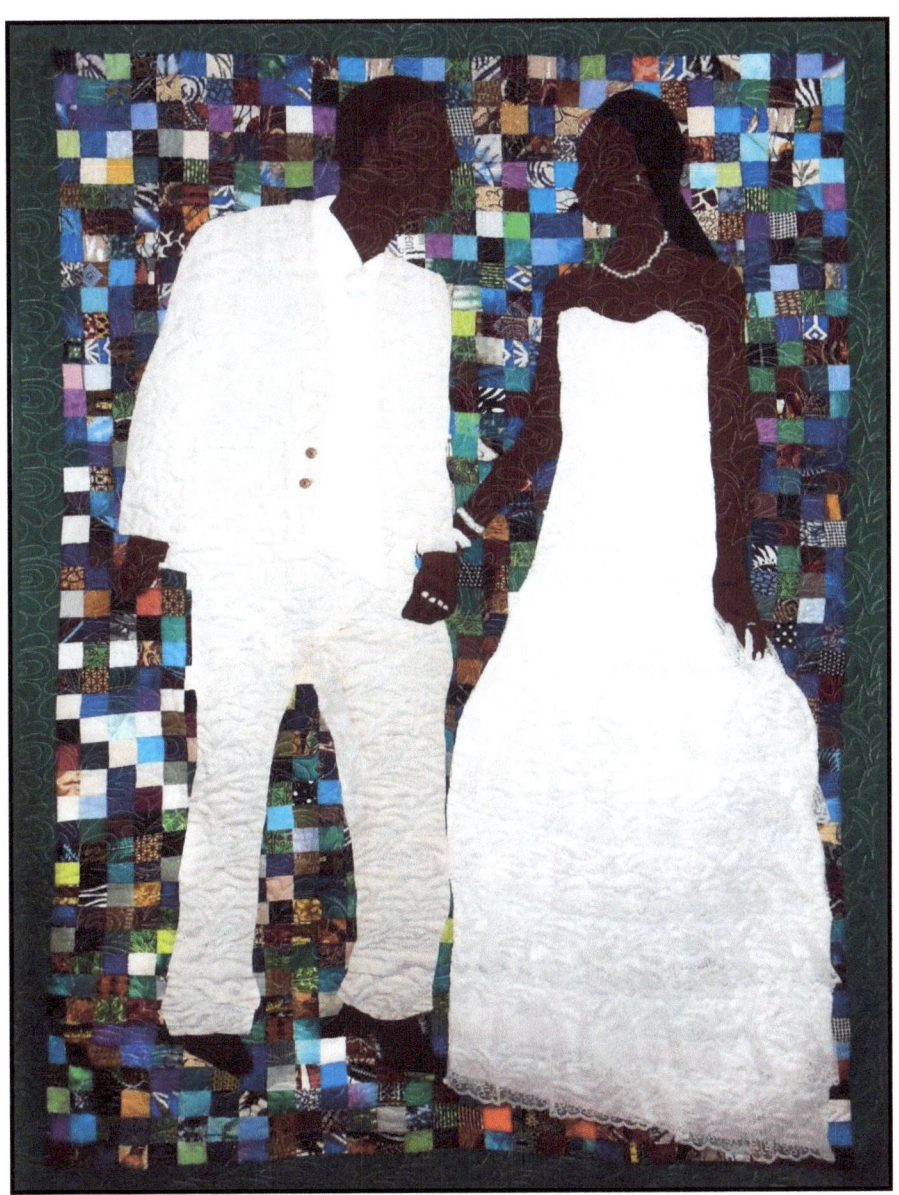

SHE IS LOVED

These quilts are an homage to weddings. I have been really fascinated by all kinds of wedding ceremonies. These quilts are just the beginning of wedding quilts to come.

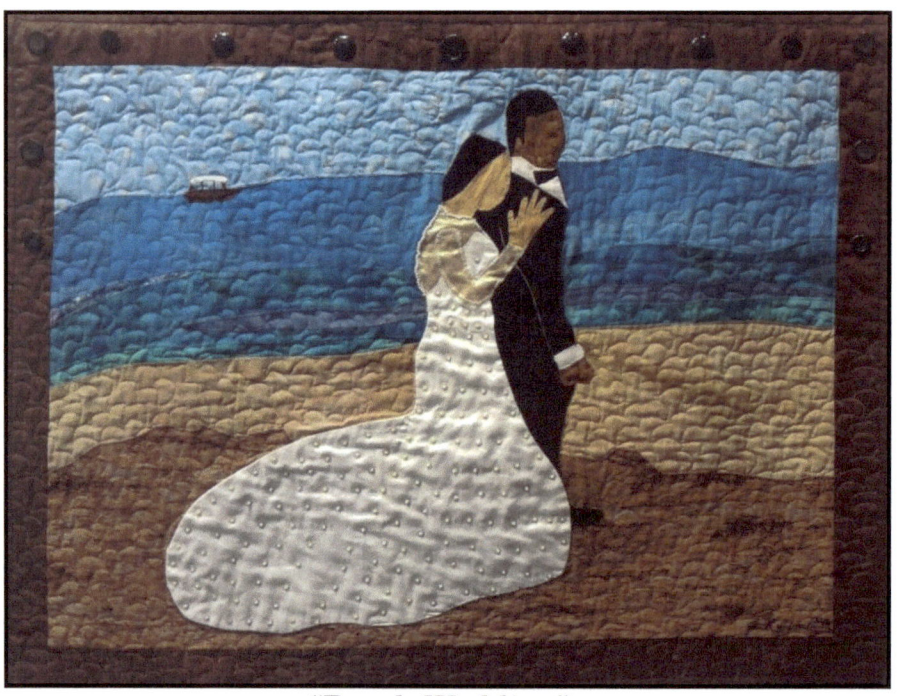

"Beach Wedding"
38" X 29"

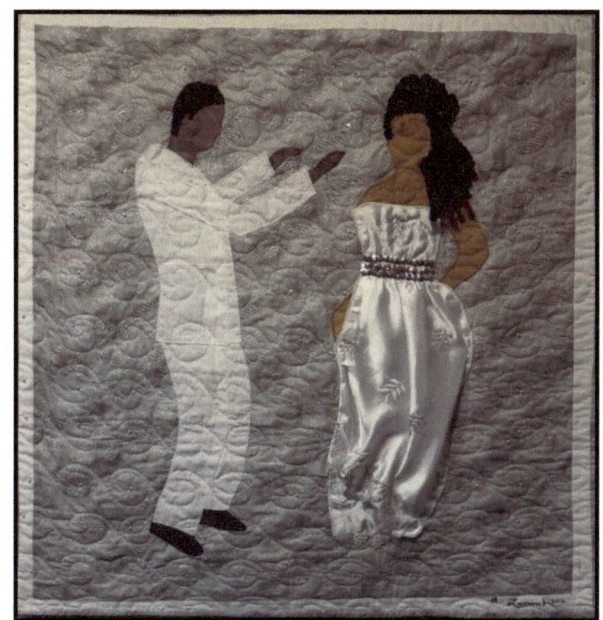

"First Dance"
28" X 32"

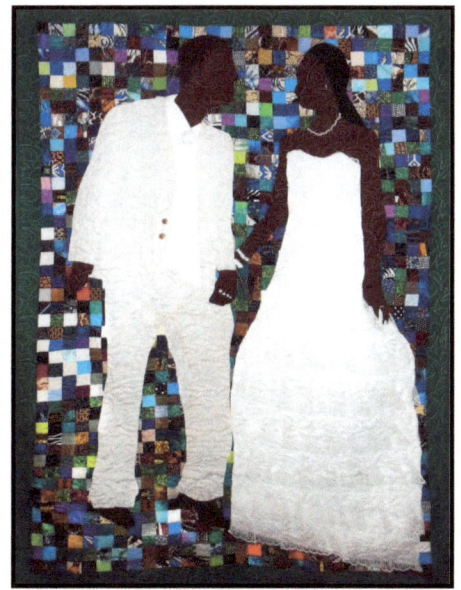

"She Said Yes"
47" X 68"

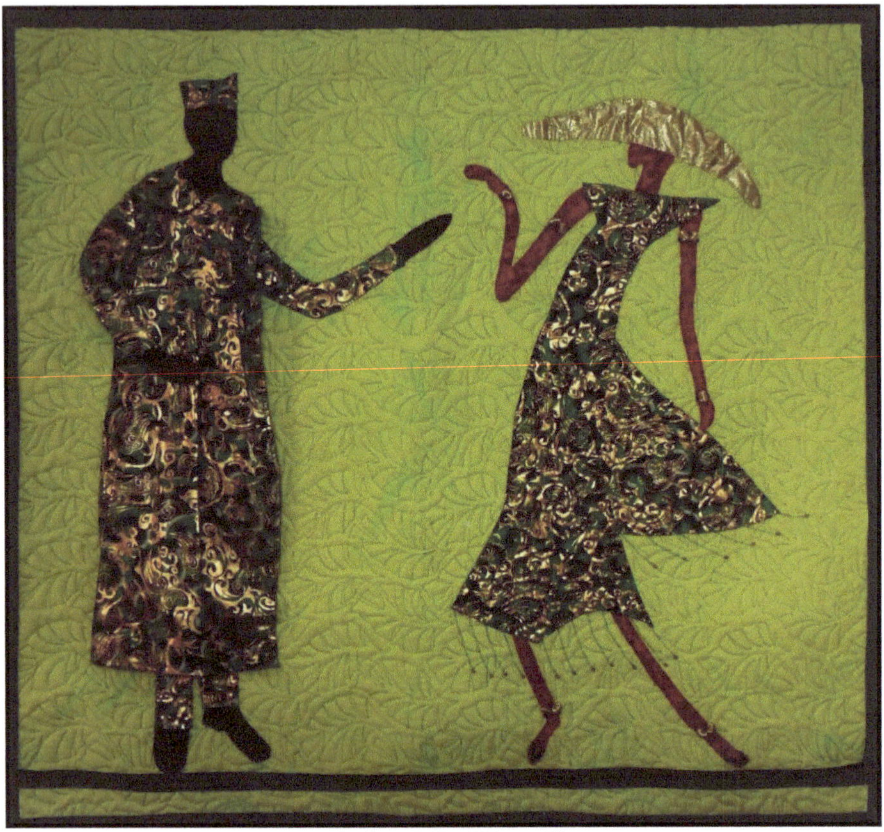

Aisha Lumumba

"Take My Hand"
49" X 40"

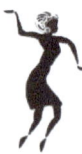

11

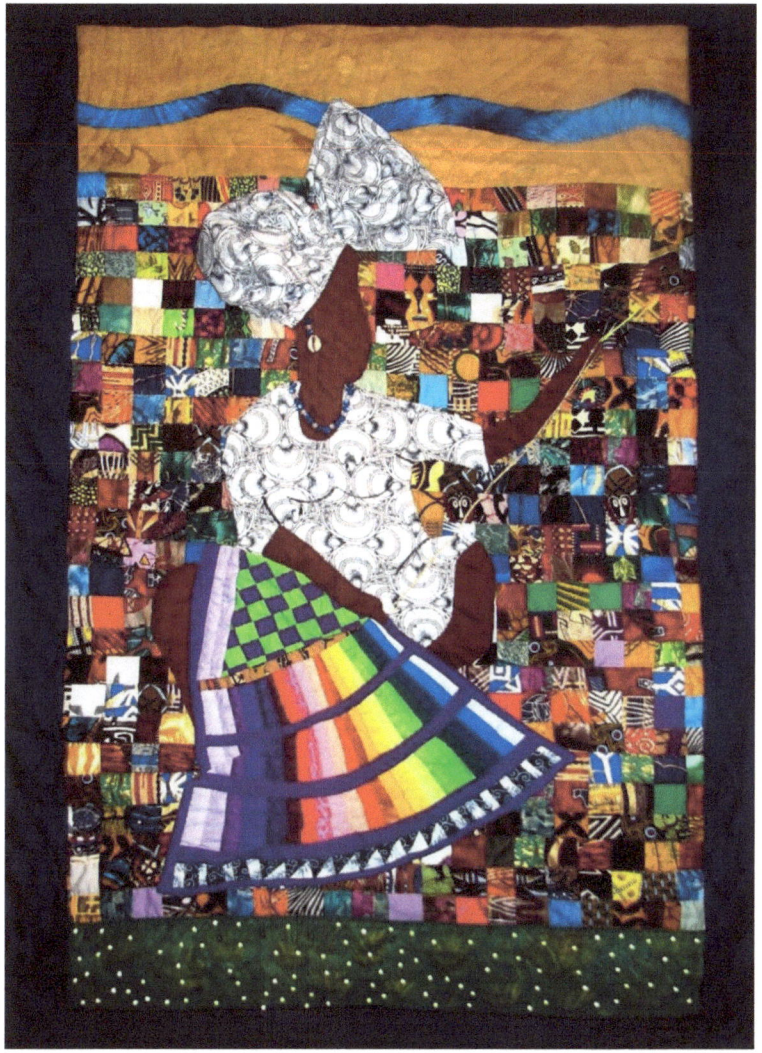

SHE IS ...

These quilts cover other ways women participate in the world. I remember a quote "Women Hold

Up Half The World." I pray that the world will eventually realize that we hold up half of it. Our contributions are equal to men, different but equal.

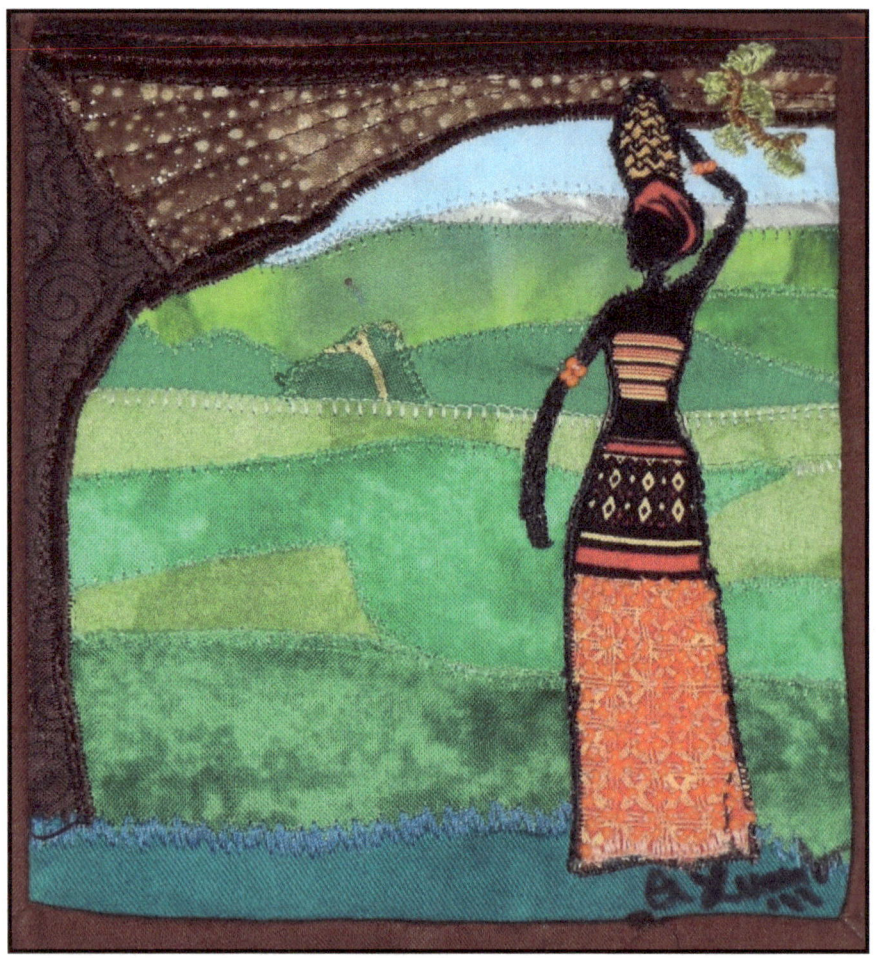

"Afternoon"
8" x 10

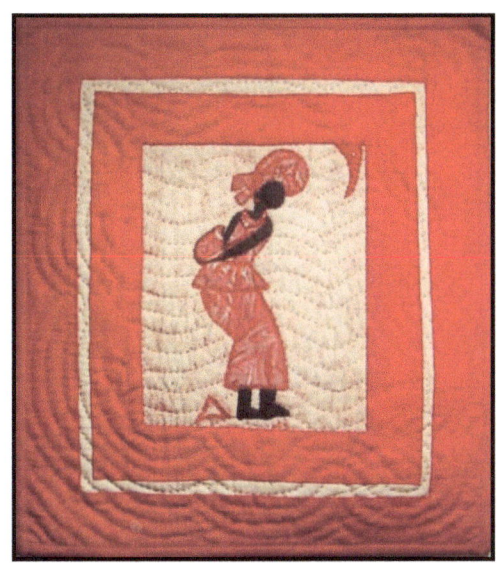

"Calabash Carrier"
15" x 17"

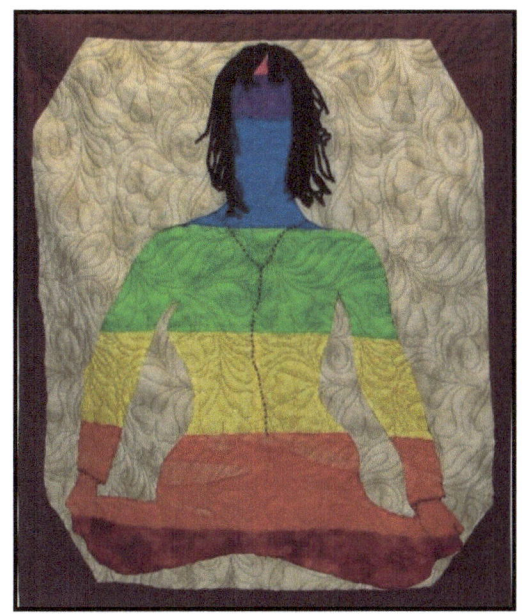

"Chakras"
46" x 55"

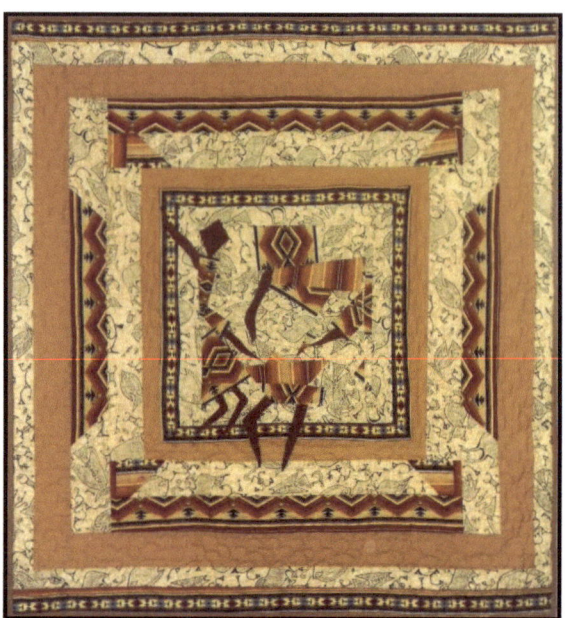

"In Motion"
36" x 40"

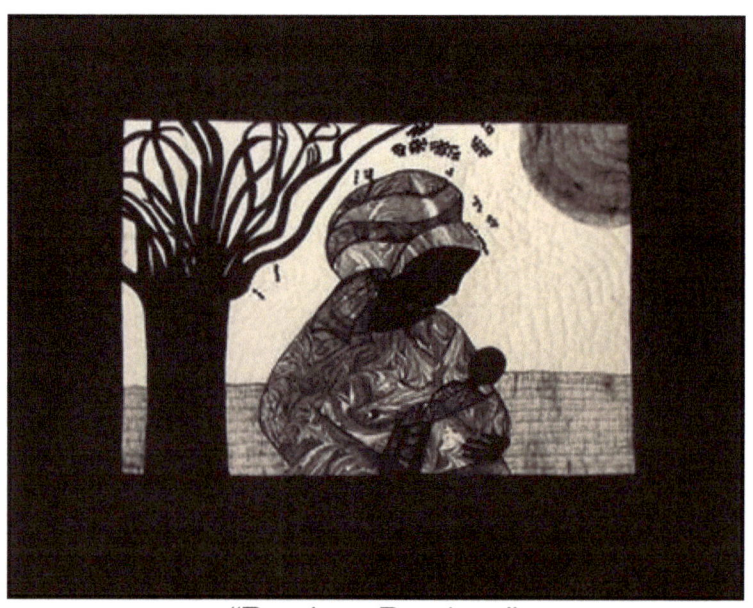

"Precious Precious"
41" x 36"

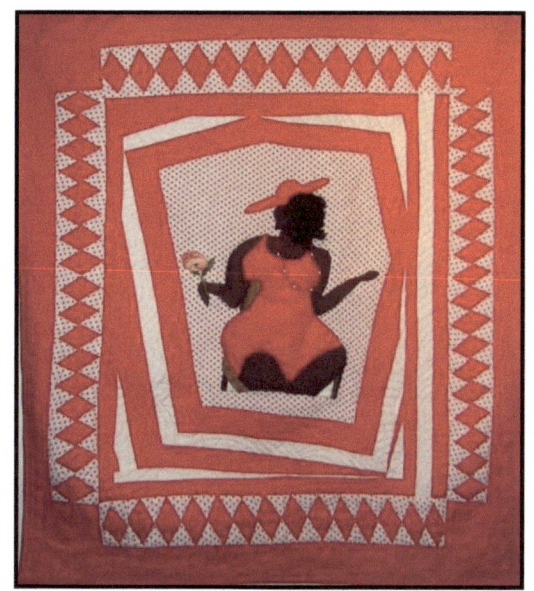

"Tough Mary
36" x 51"

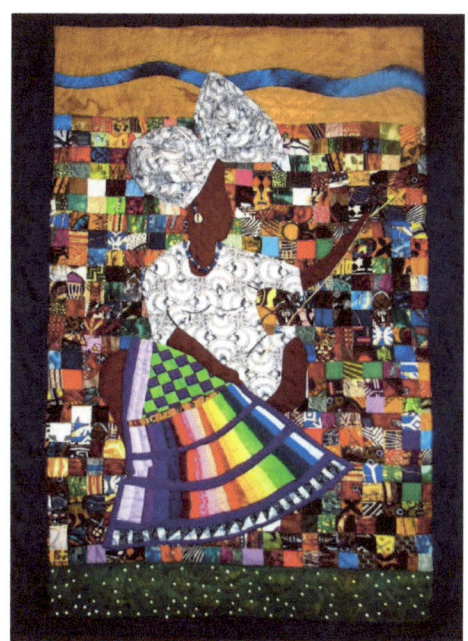

"A Quilter's Dream ... is to be one with the quilt"
36" x 53"

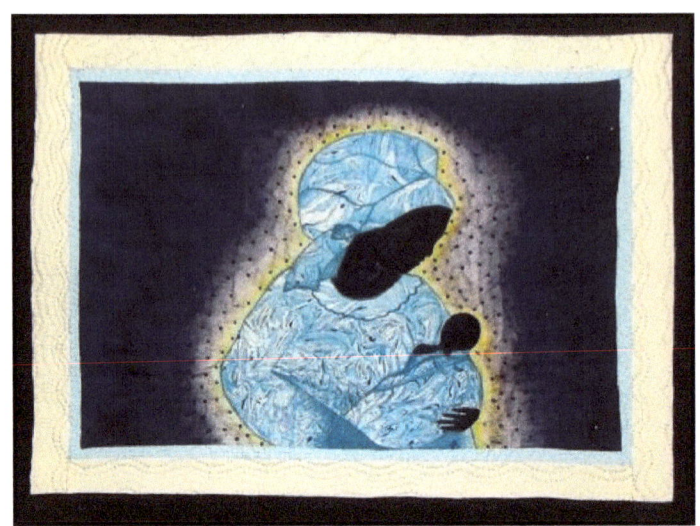

"Precious Precious 2"
41" x 36"

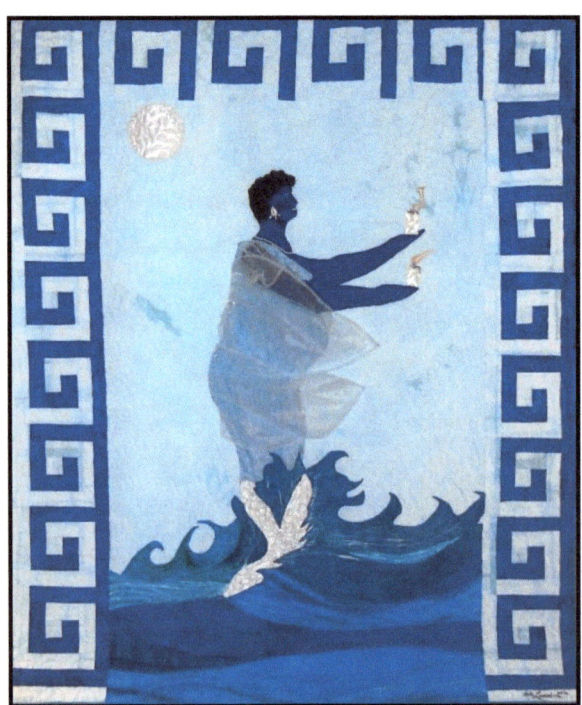

Sea Breeze
52" x 61"

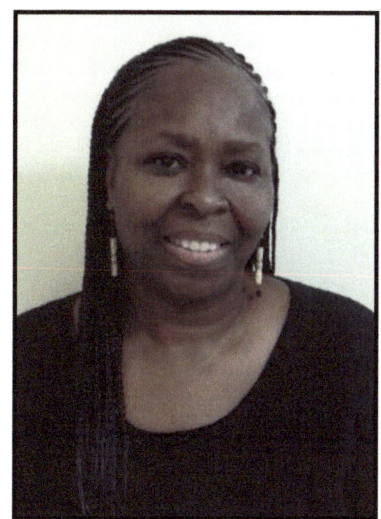

ABOUT THE AUTHOR

Aisha Lumumba is a well-known artist residing in Atlanta, Georgia USA. She was born in a rural suburb of Atlanta, known as McDonough, Georgia. She loves writing and quilting, which led her to write stories and books about quilting. Ms. Lumumba started writing in Elementary School and continues to the present day. She has more than thirty years of quilting experience, not only for practical uses, but as a form of artistic expression.

Ms. Lumumba is very prolific as a quilter and fiber artist. She started exhibiting quilts in 1983. Her quilts have appeared in more than fifty exhibits throughout the United States. Ms. Lumumba is available for Art Exhibits, Lectures, Quilt-Story Telling, Classes, Workshops, and Trunk Shows.

Her quilts are now a part of the collections of Ambassador Andrew Young, Mrs. Valerie Jackson, Dr. Stephanie Jolly, Ms. Brenda Banks, Ms. Woodie Persons, Dr. Jaulynne Dodson, The Atrium on Sweet Auburn, President & Mrs. Barack Obama and many others.

Other Titles by Aisha Lumumba

Afterwhile: The Secrets of a Woman's Heart

Cuisine on the Nile Volumes 1 and 2

Gifted: Art Quilts featuring African American History Makers

If Quilts Could Talk: My Quilts My Stories Volume 1

Scrap Easy: Building A Collage Quilt

www.obaquilts.com for more Info and Art Quilts

www.ingramcontent.com/pod-product-compliance
Lightning Source LLC
Chambersburg PA
CBHW040809200526
45159CB00022B/124